Developing a strategic mindset is an essential skill for all HR professionals. It is never too early to develop such a mindset and this book neatly shows you how.
Dr Dina Gray, strategy academic and consultant

A step-by-step roadmap on how to be a simply brilliant and fulfilled HR business partner. Eloquent, funny and thought-provoking by turn, in an age of machine learning and HR bots, it is heartening to focus on the 'human' nature of this role and how a really effective HR partner to a business area can make a transformative difference. Sage advice for all in HR, regardless of which stage they are in their career.
Sarah Stacey, Director HR Business Partnering, NATS

A compelling read for both aspiring and practicing HR business partners, written in a style that is informative and relatable and equipping those navigating the perennial challenges of this keystone HR role.
Nick Sloan, FCIPD, HR transformation specialist, management consulting industry

A great insight into strategic thinking with practical applications and a wealth of real experiences. A valuable read for all those in HR who want to make a difference.
Nigel Daly, FCIPD, HR learning and development specialist

This is an incredibly helpful, easy-to-read book with a witty slant. It provides wise advice and is an essential read for HR professionals and people leaders alike.
Rachel Gardner-Poole, Chief Operating Officer, innovation and technology sector

The HR Business Partner Handbook is one that the profession has been waiting for. It is a complete guide to understanding the depth and breadth of the role of an HR business partner and the value it can bring any organization. Coupled with expert insights from Glenn, it will help you to achieve day-to-day excellence through its informative and empowering approach as it sets out expectations to help anyone be an awesome HRBP.

Whether you're new to HR or looking to transition from a HR generalist or specialist role, this incredibly practical guide is a must-read on your journey.

Andrew Mina, People and Customer Experience Manager, HR SaaS company

This is an excellent read. It provides valuable insights, guidance and advice to someone starting out on the course of becoming an HR business partner – the sorts of insights which you don't normally get from a textbook. It gives the reader a glimpse into the author's own personal story and his views on what makes a strategic HR business partner stand out. It is thought-provoking and offers a really interesting perspective.

Elaine McIlroy, employment and immigration law firm partner

The HR Business Partner Handbook

A practical guide to being your organization's strategic people expert

Glenn Templeman

KoganPage

Publisher's note

Every possible effort has been made to ensure that the information contained in this book is accurate at the time of going to press, and the publishers and authors cannot accept responsibility for any errors or omissions, however caused. No responsibility for loss or damage occasioned to any person acting, or refraining from action, as a result of the material in this publication can be accepted by the editor, the publisher or the author.

First published in Great Britain and the United States in 2022 by Kogan Page Limited

2nd Floor, 45 Gee Street	8 W 38th Street, Suite 902	4737/23 Ansari Road
London	New York, NY 10018	Daryaganj
EC1V 3RS	USA	New Delhi 110002
United Kingdom		India

www.koganpage.com

Kogan Page books are printed on paper from sustainable forests.

ISBNs

Hardback 978 1 3986 0300 4
Paperback 978 1 3986 0298 4
Ebook 978 1 3986 0299 1

British Library Cataloguing-in-Publication Data

A CIP record for this book is available from the British Library.

Library of Congress Control Number

2021042683

Typeset by Integra Software Services, Pondicherry
Print production managed by Jellyfish
Printed and bound by CPI Group (UK) Ltd, Croydon CR0 4YY

CONTENTS

PREFACE

Before we begin this journey together, I want to take a moment to attempt to contextualize the content of this book for you as best I can. In human resources, as in life, there are many aspects of one-to-one communication that are non-verbal. Throughout this book I wish to speak to you directly and individually as if we were having coffee together. After all, what cannot be solved over coffee cannot be solved at all.

So primarily, I need you to understand that I am a person who prefers to communicate, and influence, through the medium of relationship. I do not expect anyone to heed my words unless they are already invested in the relationship with me. Which is where writing a book for people, whom I have not met and do not know, to purchase and consume is a little concerning for fear of being misunderstood. Therefore, I have expended considerable effort to articulate and present my thoughts in what I hope is a relationship-based way, the way I would to a colleague or friend. I'm treating you the same way. I want you to get to know me through the reading of this book, to understand my way of thinking, and in turn grasp the heart and intention behind the words.

Most of all, I wouldn't want you to misunderstand what I will say in the pages of this book in case you were to miss something that could be of benefit to you or those around you. I want to help you however I can. I hope in this preface I can give you a little context to set us on course to establishing our personal relationship through which I can communicate my experiences and ideas on this subject we call HR business partnering. Relationship must come before instruction.

A calling or a falling

Not many people would profess to feeling 'called' into a life as a human resources professional. In fact, most HR professionals I have spoken to throughout my career have said they simply 'fell' into human resources as if by the work of a random career selection generator, dishing out career choices at the pull of a lever. Calling aside, it does seem many of my HR colleagues have made a conscious decision at some point early in their working lives, or academic studies, to pursue a career in human resources.

Things were a little different for me. I cannot say that I 'fell' into human resources as it was instead something that I actively chose to pursue a career in *before* I entered the workplace, strange as that may sound. For me, HR was a career path that was floated whilst I was still in secondary school. Other students in a similar position considering future career choices will more often select doctor, firefighter, police officer, engineer, or of course for a younger cohort, astronaut! Seldom if ever would you hear a young person say they wish to become a human resources professional when they grow up! For me, I did not want to be any of those things, but by the time I was finishing secondary school I did know one thing for certain – whatever I were to do next, working with people would be my main aim and the most important factor of any career choices.

Throughout my life up to that point, I had not been particularly excellent at mathematics, science or anything of that sort, but instead, to put it simply, I was good at people. In my case this manifested not only in having a wide group of friends but also being comfortable with befriending the full spectrum of people in my sphere. The realization that there was a 'people' profession, a career in 'being good at people' so I thought, made HR (or personnel as it was still often referred to back then) the ideal fit for my lifetime aspirations of 'working with people'. Little did I know how these simplistic ideas would all play out more than 20 years later.

In the writing of this book, my thoughts and ideas are not constructed from a place that I happened upon by pure chance or happy coincidence. Instead, the ideas presented for you in this book are the result of a sense of vocation, a feeling of calling, borne out of a genuine, natural and unforced interest in people as my perpetual motivation. Nothing is interesting to me without people in the equation.

I am, at the very least, an advocate for human resources professionals, but I have personally discovered that I am also really rather biased towards my belief in the absolute benefit to the business world of perfectly constructed HR business partners. My belief in the power of a good HR business partner is unrivalled, there are no limits to what they can achieve where people are concerned.

Therefore, this book is not intended to be an even-handed theoretical study of the pros and cons of the role of HR business partners, although it does go some way toward that. Instead I hope you find it to be a somewhat biased and entirely partisan view of the very essential role a valuable HR business partner plays in business. It is my own love letter to HR business partners everywhere and I make no apologies for that. Hopefully, as a reader of this book you weren't expecting anything less!

I felt it important to spell these things out here, as I expect many moments of bias towards the virtues of the HR business partner will emerge throughout the reading of this book. Consider yourself forewarned!

Although, more importantly, I believe that understanding each other is paramount in cultivating a vibrant people profession. Therefore, I hope as you read this you will begin to understand that my belief in the value of the HR business partner is borne out of a genuine interest in people, and a fundamental principle that having a human responsible for the interests of other humans in business is an imperative that none of us can afford to overlook.

By that I mean, I hope you find my prejudiced campaign for the case of the HR business partner to be an honourable one, on the basis it ultimately has its roots in a good thing – a desire to see businesses thrive because they contain people who know the true value of other humans.

Qualifiers

Before we go any further, I need to underline some key points that shape everything I will set out from here on in.

Firstly, I want you to read this as if it is a draft or an unfinished work. Reading in this way will allow you the space to consider your own personal thoughts and ideas throughout the text. I have tried to create a figurative conversation between you and me as author and reader. Throughout this book I will implicitly be asking, 'does this help?' and 'am I missing anything?' By doing this I aim to open a kind of virtual dialogue so you can also input to these points, adding and subtracting to what I will set out in this book.

Secondly, I will remind us throughout that the chapters and sections in this book are principles; they are not an exhaustive list. Inevitably, much is left unsaid. It is very hard to set out how all of us should always be and do in every situation facing us. Hence throughout, I will illustrate principles with only occasional reference to methods that I have personally used and found to be useful.

Finally, on qualifiers, I must caution that all my experiences have been lived, sometimes painfully, from within businesses. I have always been an 'in-house' HR professional. I have no consultancy experience prior to writing this book. Therefore, I have always lived and breathed the HR function, the organization and all their foibles. My thoughts and ideas have been formed by this experience of being 'in-house', for better or for worse.

For all of you

This book is about HR business partners, written for HR business partners by an HR business partner. But maybe this book is not for you. If you are already an HR business partner then I hope it's not for you, my hope is that you already know and can apply everything I'm about to say and that this book is therefore a mildly amusing allegory of your working life so far as an HR professional. My aim is to construct valuable HR business partners, so if you have already reached that rare accolade in your career journey you need read no further.

Throughout the writing of this book my mind has often been on guiding entry-level HR professionals through the long journey of becoming a valuable and fully competent HR business partner. Given that even the most gifted person can expect this journey to take a good many years, throughout the book I have inevitably turned my attention to the needs of HR business partners at many different points of this journey towards valuable competence.

Therefore, my hope is that the contents of this book can speak to the entire HR business partner cadre, irrespective of levels of experience or distance travelled on the journey. Having walked this journey myself, and lived through the highs and lows, I hope I have been wise enough to learn a little about what is needed from the perennial HR business partner at all points on the journey.

Of particular note, I have observed there to be at least two key points where people get 'stuck' on the HR business partner spectrum and I have tried to focus particular attention on these two areas to enable readers to become unstuck (or to not get stuck in the first place). They are: 1) the transition from advisory roles to business partnering roles; and 2) operating effectively at the strategic level.

For the experienced HR business partner, I hope you find something amusing, and above all, useful. Also, perhaps that I have managed to put into words all the things you know to be true about what makes you successful but that no one has ever spelled out – a glimmer of recognition of the factors that make the HR business partner successful.

Also, I could not conclude this section without mentioning one other people group. This book is also written for all the people who, diligently adhering to strict social etiquette (or not managing to muster anything more creative to ask), have ever asked me, 'what do you do?', and have then responded to the answer of 'HR', with a blank-stare pause, causing me to clarify, 'human resources'. This answer always seems to be met with that polite only half-concealed further blank-gaze-look of not knowing quite what that entails or what to say next. Either that, or people generally think to themselves, 'oh, how terrible', or worse, they think nothing at all, but are too polite to say. Even those that purport to know something and kindly offer, 'oh, hiring and firing', to which I reluctantly am forced to respond in the positive using the reciprocal social etiquette – I hope this book is for you too.

Now, hopefully, everyone will have a better idea of what an HR business partner *really* does.

Correct me if I am wrong

Wherever you sit on this spectrum, there is one subject relevant to all which I have come to believe in that I do not cover later in this book – it is something I recognize as the 'power of disagreement'. The 'power of disagreement' is each of us recognizing the power we have in ourselves over our own mind. It is not a requirement that we must always agree with each other on all things (or equally that we must always disagree). Being human and being able to sit down and think, and thereby conclude on whether we agree or disagree, is the platform that provides us with a future course of action.

So firstly, my hope as you read this is that what I have written validates what you are already thinking and doing as an HR professional. My second hope for you as you read this book is that it makes you think, and that such thinking would lead you to consider the power of disagreement. I wish that many more people would take the time to just think a little more and consider for themselves what it is they really think and why they think it. Whether the contents of this book are something you can agree with (which will therefore hopefully validate or change your future actions and behaviours), or whether there are some parts you disagree with (which therefore will ultimately augment and improve the work I have put into this book), there is power in the mind of the reader not just the writer.

The 'how' of HR

If, however, you sit in a subtly different camp and you're reading this book because you have an interest in starting a career in human resources, then I hope that this book helps equip you for the journey.

Starting out in HR you will learn a lot of the 'what' either on the job or as part of an accredited qualification, or both; however, what I saw was lacking within the myriad of HR teaching is 'how' we do it all.

Therefore, in writing this book I have specifically focused on what I know and understand to be the 'how' of HR business partnering. I will unpack the 'how' continuously throughout this book. As you might expect, and as I have indeed discovered, much of the 'how' is transferable to any corporate 'business partner' role, whether it be in finance, business planning or other internal business support functions.

So, rest assured, the details of 'what' the HR profession must do will be set out in the workplace, in academia, or in other important texts. Here we will pursue that which is missing elsewhere, those things that no one ever really tells you but nevertheless expects that you will master somehow seemingly by a cosmical osmosis. Finally, I hope that I have recorded these important 'hows' not only in one place but also in some form of logical order that aligns to your own personal career journey.

Laugh, think, cry

Humans really are brilliant and can do incredible things, and mostly I find the highest value in what we can teach each other through the experiences of life. One of my favourite life teachers was Jim Valvano, affectionately known as Jimmy V. Jimmy was an American college basketball coach, most notably at North Carolina State university (NC State).

Sadly, Jimmy lost his battle with cancer on 28 April 1993. Life may sometimes be short, but our words have the power to last forever and in a now-immortalized acceptance speech for the Arthur Ashe courage and humanitarian award at the 1993 Excellence in Sports Performance Yearly Award (ESPY), Jimmy gave advice for life that is relevant to all of us today.

You can watch the full video online (The V Foundation for Cancer Research, 2008). The point that holds pertinence to me personally, and has become Jimmy's legacy long after his death, is below:

> When people say to me, how do you get through life or each day? It's the same thing. To me, there are three things we all should do every day. We should do this every day of our lives.
>
> - No 1 is laugh. You should laugh every day.
>
> - No 2 is think. You should spend some time in thought.
>
> - No 3 is you should have your emotions moved to tears, could be happiness or joy.
>
> But think about it. If you laugh, you think and you cry, that's a full day. That's a heck of a day. You do that seven days a week, you're going to have something special.

Jimmy may have lost the battle, but he did not lose the war – his words transcend time and make their way to us today.

Why is this incredible? Because in our profession we're dealing with the business of people every day and people have the power to impact who we are and what we do with every one of those days. We should remember that fact the next time we roll into 'just another' meeting.

I also think working in human resources is a little like this: each day of our work we should remember to laugh, we should think and sometimes it is ok to have our emotions moved to tears too. After all, we are in the business of people and these are real lives we are working with each day.

In that same speech Jimmy goes on to say, 'I always have to think about what's important in life to me are these three things. Where you started, where you are and where you're going to be.'

Again, these words are deeply relevant to us as HR professionals who in our roles have a responsibility for the career journeys of others. Moreover, we're human too, so in reading this book I hope it enables you to consider where you started, where you are today and, ultimately, where you are headed.

And finally

I should also mention at the outset that whilst I have always tended to take myself and what I do very seriously, I also have a sense of humour, so I hope that you catch it within the pages of this book!

I wanted to write something that I would enjoy reading myself, which was also true to real life, so I've weaved as much humour throughout as I would in my day-to-day working life. If something sounds a little over the top or does not fit with the expected flow of the text, it's probably meant to be a joke!

In my professional life I am always serious on the surface and human at heart.

Reference

The V Foundation for Cancer Research (2008) Jim's 1993 ESPY Speech (video) https://youtu.be/HuoVM9nm42E (archived at https://perma.cc/KF6Y-5F52)

Introduction

A well-trodden path should be easy to follow

As to methods there may be a million and then some, but principles are few. The man who grasps principles can successfully select his own methods. The man who tries methods, ignoring principles, is sure to have trouble.

HARRINGTON EMERSON (1911)

The guiding rails

Having spent my whole career with HR people, and of course being one myself, it seems to me that despite the many and myriad business theories we operate with each day, the common HR business partner really does not have an underpinning set of principles for how we should perform the mechanics of our role.

This leaves many HR people whom I've met to flounder around in their approach to being an HR business partner, focusing instead on values such as honesty, integrity, credibility and professionalism (whatever that word means to whomever), or worst of all, 'leading by example'. If it were up to me, I would strike this last phrase from our people lexicon altogether. Leading by example is not a value as the phrase does not have any clearly defined attributes other than hoping others will take your lead. There are spectrums of 'example' that can be set, from visionary to inappropriate, so when considering values, the important point is really what we stand for and what principles we will live by.

As already mentioned in the Preface, when considering the even less discussed topic of principles, most of us therefore become like a train without the track – we are often aware of a destination and stops on the way but getting there becomes much harder, or impossible in some cases, because we really have no rails to guide us day-to-day between stations. We still move in the general direction of our desired destination(s), but progress is much slower and more painful than it ought to be. Unfortunately, there are too many HR advisors who are stuck and never manage to progress past this first- or second-line advisory stage.

The issue of principles can be particularly acute with individuals who have the title, or the expectations bestowed upon them, of being 'strategic' or 'senior', and of course for all who aspire to those roles.

If you have not yet been required to become 'strategic', please be on notice that it is coming. There is only so long that HR can use humans to do excellent policy, process and advice until automation, systemization and/or bots will replace what we used to do so averagely. Technology will continue to narrow the window in which humans can add value to the business of being human.

An awful lot is lost, or never actually gained, in the transition from an HR role performing advice to one performing strategic activities. This transition usually takes the form of a 'natural progression' from advisor to business partner, or business partner to strategic/senior business partner. If you've been around a reasonably sized HR team for more than a couple of minutes you will recognize this well-established 21st century HR paradigm. I believe this practice is at the root of the misapplication, or misunderstanding, of HR business partnering as defined by Ulrich in his book, *Human Resource Champions* (1997).

The word 'strategic' can be difficult to define in HR. Not just for the individuals performing these important strategic roles, it is particularly difficult at times for the individual, the directors or managers, and collectively, the whole organization or set of service users to define what they really want and need from an HR person purporting to be strategic.

Proof of this point lies in the words of many organizations when advertising for one of these strategic HR roles. Job adverts frequently list the principal accountabilities of their 'strategic' or 'senior' HR business partners to be 'operational', 'tactical' and a version of 'comfortable with managing casework effectively'. This fact is quite possibly one of the single most annoying things about working in HR. It is of vital importance that we start to understand the separation between operational and strategic, and once that is well understood then start to apply it consistently throughout our profession. Solving this problem will resolve many other daily issues that are caused by this root problem, the most prevalent of which being that 'strategic HR business partners' do not have enough capacity to do 'strategic' things because of being bogged down in more immediate operational-type work. I will specifically address this problem in Part Three of this book, 'The road to strategic'.

Clearly, when considered at large these (operational, tactical etc) are roles performed at the policy, process and product level, not at a strategic level. I am yet to encounter any strategic casework. Complex, yes, small 's' strategically important, yes, but not casework that's part of a wider organizational strategy. If you have, then please let me know! Figure 0.1 gives a simple view of the strategy, policy and processes levels referred to here. The figure should be read from the top down, with vision guiding strategy, policies in line with the strategy and processes to deliver the aligned policies.

FIGURE 0.1   Strategy pyramid

SOURCE Glenn Templeman (2014)

Is it possible therefore, that whole organizations, businesses and enterprises still do not know what strategic input from people-experts looks like?

Continuing with the earlier point, this is never more visible than in the job adverts that are routinely placed for the plethora of roles with titles concerning HR business partnering.

These adverts often appear to be asking for an individual who can operate at a senior level after many years' experience in our field, commanding the most elite skillsets in the HR discipline, but who is then also required to simultaneously perform transactional-policy-following and basic administrative processes. This is almost always what is meant by 'prepared to take a hands-on approach' or versions thereof. It is deeply perplexing as to why we would want a high-level strategic change initiator to also wind back the career clock and master local administrative processes (and why we would want to pay a premium for them to do it!).

There is hope though. Within the profession there are many useful texts and theories that guide the 'what' and 'why' of HR practice. These professional and academic works are usually well known and widely used and can guide those seeking to understand 'what' to do in the strategic HR space. This is where, as HR business partners, we often see the same or similar interventions rolled out at different organizations (nine-box grids for example!). As a profession we can sometimes rely solely on these strategic activities to define our strategic people-expert offering. As if *doing* strategic things is better than first *being* a strategic people-expert. In order to *be* strategic, we must understand 'how' we should partner with a business. Although we are flush with the 'what' I find we are somewhat bereft of corresponding 'how' actions. There is little of note, professional or academic, to teach us 'how' we should partner with a business.

I have discovered that this area of 'how' one should be an HR business partner is either seen as not important or entirely overlooked in favour of delivering a hamster wheel of 'what' activities. Often, the best we can manage in 'how' to partner with a business is to state overall aims, such as, 'you need to become their trusted advisor'. Or in a development setting we offer statements such as, 'you just need to take a more holistic approach'. Too often we only have common retorts for very real and specific challenges. It is this specific challenge of being a true strategic partner where we need the most help to ensure we do not become entirely unstuck.

At best, this strategic partner challenge will occur in a forward-thinking business that challenges its HR people to add more to the organization through strategic input and intervention. At worst, the challenge is laid down through the restructuring of the HR function and prefixing the job titles of a bunch of the longest serving people with the word 'strategic'. Unfortunately, the latter is surprisingly common for many HR functions. This process literally yields people who are strategic in name only. This back-to-front approach might stand some chance of success, on occasion, if we had a clear and consistent application of 'becoming a strategic partner' that could be rolled out to enable people to succeed in this scenario. The CIPD HR profession map (CIPD, 2013) has helped greatly in this area by setting out the eight behaviours that identify how professionals need to carry out their activities and contribute to organizational success. However, there is still more road to travel and more people to consistently heed the message.

The glass ceiling

The pivotal moment in most HR generalists' careers is that seemingly impossible transition from advisor/consultant/junior or operational level role (or any other ambiguous designation of a transactional and or purely advisory role) to a strategic role, be it explicitly or implicitly stated in the role title (senior, strategic, executive and principal are a few common prefixes). Breaking through this glass ceiling can seem impossible until the moment the stars align, and a seat opens up and all other competition are absent. There must be another way.

Organizations do often tend to trust what they know in this field of people. This is not a rule but more of an observation made over time that where it is possible to hire internally to business partner, it is probable. This has an obvious list of pros and cons that I will not deal with here, but suffice to say it makes the issue of transition, and the matter of how to be a business partner, all the more important to get right.

I do believe there to be a general trend of promoting internally from advisor to partner within organizations. That was the route by which I achieved my first proper business partner title (and role) and I've seen many others also make this transition internally. I struggled for years myself with this definite transition and I see this regularly across HR everywhere I go. It was the principal reason for writing this book. I found myself long into my HR career and still encountering good and talented people experiencing this same problem.

In the best cases there is specific training for HR advisors over and above the well-trodden on-the-job learning. Usually some kind of organizational design and development training or perhaps some specific leadership programme is made available.

However, too often the appointment, or transformation, to the new role is expected to produce magical results in itself, as if by taking the reins off and requiring flight by virtue of a job title will be enough to make it so. Seldom does this produce decent results in the step up from advisor to partner (unless the individual has long since been operating at the partner level just without the title). It seems that busting through this glass ceiling is only the first step in becoming a strategic level practitioner.

Learning the 'how'

The 'what' of business partnering is usually self-evident within an organization. There is always an element of, 'we want you to go over there to be with them and do that'. We focus heavily on the 'what', with good reason because this leads to the development of skills and knowledge for the business partner as well as providing the services we offer – it also keeps us busy and therefore serves to answer the business's 'what are you doing to justify your cost?' question (more on that to come).

So, for example, the applied theory seems to be that delivering talent management and succession planning initiatives within a business area will hopefully begin to develop that organizational development skill and knowledge within the business partner (at the very least we will know how to work the process next time). This example is often repeated and termed as 'learning by doing' or 'learning on the job'.

All valid practices of course, but it starts to expose what is excluded in the pursuit of mastering the 'what' of HR business partnering. This well-established business practice has created the void, or rather created HR business partners who are devoid, of coherent and effective principles that can be applied in all situations however much or little is known.

As a function, focusing on the 'what' also helps us to quantify workload and tick off important tasks as and when they are complete. These are tangible measurements in a profession that often adds a lot of value through the intangible. This is both a reference to the clarity of 'what' HR does as well as the importance of making tangible the principles of 'how' it does 'what' it does. Even in the age of measurement, intangible has its benefits too.

The business case

Our people are our biggest asset. This sounds good, is trotted out often and is usually true, but people within a business are seldom treated as we would hope to treat an asset.

An asset is something that contains underlying value and can therefore grow in value over time and can be used to generate further value in the future (usually in the form of income). In short, an asset is something that pays you to hold it, not something that costs you to hold it.

Of course, this statement about people being the biggest asset is not always completely true for some businesses or for all parts of a business (even if people are usually a business's *biggest* cost!). In some cases, it can be intellectual property rights (IPR) that is the biggest asset, or it could be a tangible asset such as specialist computers, software, machinery or real estate.

I think it is important to acknowledge the paradox here: people are involved in the design, production and ongoing maintenance of all these assets, so it may be true that the people are still the biggest asset, but it could also be true that the people required are 'commodities' in service of the true asset. Both competing points can be true, usually at different moments in the life cycle or supply chain of the business.

That aside, in the United Kingdom in the 21st century, we have a strong tendency towards services in our business offerings meaning that people, at whatever point in the chain, are likely an important if not our most important asset. At the very least, people are an asset of some sort at some point to all businesses regardless of sector, industry or product. If this can be seen to be true, we must surely need some deep expertise to help businesses to maintain, develop and shore up the future growth of this asset so that it does what an asset is meant to do, which is to hold underlying value, appreciate and generate more income.

A business would expect deep technical knowledge and competence from other disciplines in order to preserve and grow the value of its IPR, IT or physical assets and so it should be the same with its people assets.

I think the monetary analogy of an asset is useful here because there is a direct connection to many of the publicly and privately owned and traded businesses to which we are referring, or indeed any business with aspirations to become publicly owned and traded in future.

The Standard & Poor's (S&P) index of the 500 largest companies by capitalization grows by an average of 9.6 per cent per year, which it has done over the past 91 years (Damodaran, 2020). If you do not know anything about stocks and money markets, take it from me that 91 years is as reliable a reference period as any of us have.

In some years the index will contract but in other years it will grow by more than 10 per cent, creating the 10 per cent average overall. This means that, on average, the 500 or so companies within the index see their share price grow by an average of 10 per cent each year. I am simplifying for the purposes of our analogy; companies will drop in and out of the index due to their overall capitalization, so some will inevitably fail to see this kind of consistent sustained growth in value.

There are a number of ways we could develop this analogy to demonstrate the point (which I hope we are getting by now), but I think the simplest is to say that if I buy shares in an S&P 500 index fund, and I hold those shares for a fair number of years, I have the absolute expectation that I will be getting a 10 per cent return on my money invested. No ifs, no buts.

Additionally, I expect not only the growth of the underlying value of my investment by 10 per cent per year but also the annual or quarterly dividend payment that is rightfully mine as a partial owner of the monies earned and generated by this asset. An owner in these terms not only benefits from the underlying growth in value of the asset but also regular payments of portions of the profit generated in accordance with the corresponding ownership percentage.

If we are keeping track, this means that if I reinvest the periodic dividend I receive I'm going to grow my asset at a rate of more than 10 per cent per year. There are of course experts in the financial field who will claim to be able to outperform this market average. We must remember to remain focused on being people-experts who can offer our business leaders extraordinary people performance.

Monetary detour complete, the salient point is that individuals and businesses in a capitalist society are committed absolutely in working to achieve the growth of their own value. In pursuit of this 'value', it is conceivable that these 500 businesses might cite their 'people' as their biggest asset and may coincidentally also have HR functions to ensure that their biggest asset is being suitably looked after. To this point, I would assert that it is people, not money, that makes the world go around.

Having worked myself within the not-for-profit, charity and governmental sectors this manifests itself here too. In charities and not-for-profits there's always a growth revenue target, a financial fundraising goal or a strategically important project with a fundamental funding element. It is no different, in my view, to the business world where there are a range of EBIT (earnings before interest and tax) targets and financial stretch goals.

Government is different, however, but even here post-2008 financial crisis it was firmly about how to do more with less, a more nuanced type of value growth. In monetary terms this would be called looking for a 'higher yield', a greater expectation of return on investment.

HR knows best

If all of what I have said here is true, or if we can recognize truth within it, what does it mean for us?

What should be required of a people-expert-business-partner in order to drive the type of growth we know is expected from business? Moreover, how can a business, charity, not-for-profit or government organization afford to misunderstand the benefit of the people-expert-business-partner role?

It seems in the quest to understand and to justify how HR adds value to the business (HR is a non-income-generating overhead after all), the business quantifies HR only by what the business already understands about HR. Ironically, it is the functions that only the deep people-expert can understand and articulate that truly add the greatest value to an organization. Only a competent people-expert can demonstrate the depths of value HR can add to a business.

This recognizable paradigm creates a kind of mind-bending paradox where HR business partners, rather than being revered and trusted thought leaders in the sphere of people, can be reduced to something far more administrative in a reductive quest for understanding and easily quantifying 'what the HR business partner does' and how HR 'adds value'.

This paradigm can often lead onto probably one of the most frustrating challenges for us as professionals – the self-justified chief executive/director/manager that says 'I'm human so I know about people' challenge. This is a frustrating but prevalent condition where people apply a thought process based on the unspoken theory of 'I'm a human so therefore I understand other humans, I know how they feel, think, react, so I don't have much use for a people-expert because, by definition, I am one'. This is a big blocker to successfully managing complex people issues. This type of leader will always struggle to defer to the people profession to lead the organization's professional approach to people. As the saying goes, 'Why have a dog and bark yourself?' This is a sobering reminder for us that the accolade of people-expert must be earned and not granted.

Ultimately, I occasionally become alarmingly concerned that businesses just do not expect enough of their HR business partners, but seem content with someone they can trust who will mostly do what they want to a reasonable level of competence. If we can weed out this kind of settling-for-average apathy firstly from our businesses and secondly from our profession, then we will have a much more successful and bright future ahead of us. Not to mention, far more interesting work to do.

Instead of this leaning toward mediocrity, there should be more business leaders who are secretly wondering how their HR business partner knows more about the future of their business than they do.

References

CIPD (2013) *CIPD Profession Map*, Chartered Institute of Personnel and Development [online] https://peopleprofession.cipd.org/profession-map (archived at https://perma.cc/H4NG-7B65)

Damodaran, A (2020) *Historical Returns on Stocks, Bonds and Bills: 1928–2020*, Stern Business School New York University [online] http://pages.stern.nyu.edu/~adamodar/New_Home_Page/datafile/histretSP.html (archived at https://perma.cc/427E-J9T2)

Emerson, H (1911) *The Clothier and Furnisher*, 78 (6), The Convention: Fifteenth annual convention of the National Association of Clothiers, held June 5 and 6, 1911, George N Lowry Company, New York

Ulrich, D (1997) *Human Resource Champions: The next agenda for adding value and delivering results*, Harvard Business School Press, Boston

PART ONE

The foundational structure

Having talked already about the gap in the 'how' of HR business partnering, we must first pause and reference the importance of the 'what'. This book deals with the 'how', but that does not mean to entirely cast aside the 'what'.

Throughout I will make the general assumption that to be an HR business partner we must already have mastered the 'what' of HR practice. Whether that includes appropriate levels of qualifications, a depth of working experience or other inputs, the main point is that the knowledge must be there. I'll expound this point in Chapter 1.

To begin building success and longevity, 'The foundational structure' is required to ground us in the right things and to enable additional necessary building blocks of competence to be added. These building blocks cannot be skipped over or built later. These parts are set out in a sequential order. It is an order that I believe to be very natural in the development and progression of an HR business partner. It is also, I believe, a very logical order – when building a house, we cannot tile the roof without first completing walls to hold it up. In the same way, an HR business partner cannot undertake strategic activity without first becoming competent in all aspects of HR. Without the cornerstone the whole house will fall apart.

As a reminder, these foundations are principles and do not represent an exhaustive list. 'The foundational structure' is a three-part model, each part carrying weight and importance. Everything we do will hang on the effective and consistent performance of these three foundations.

01

Knowing HR

Why we do the 'what'

So what is the starting point for being an HR business partner? Well of course, it could only be one thing, which is the comprehensive knowledge of human resources – 'knowing HR' if you will.

If we do not have the knowledge required to be a competent HR generalist, then we cannot be an advocate for HR practice and therefore cannot be an HR business partner or become a people-expert to the business. It is really this simple. This knowledge is a prerequisite for becoming an HR business partner.

In my view, this is a pure point and there really is not much clarification required, except perhaps on the definition of 'competent'. I deem the award of the title of 'competent' to be high praise indeed. Therefore, the 'competent' individual who becomes an HR business partner is already by default an experienced authority on the matters of HR practice. The HR generalist will have knowledge that spans the entire sphere of people-related activity across the universe of people practice. They will know something about everything (or a little about a lot, if you prefer that definition).

A competent individual will already likely be experienced in HR process, systems and products, with an intimate understanding of how they work and, most crucially, *why* they are performed. Understanding why these functions are performed might sound obvious – who would perform an action without truly understanding why they are performing it? However, I have discovered that expecting everyone to always understand why we in HR are doing something can be somewhat fanciful. Herein lies a key difference between the title of 'HR business partner', and the knowledge applied by a real and certifiable people-expert-business-partner.

The fundamental component to 'knowing HR' is not just knowing *what* HR does but *why* it does those things. Understanding why is the difference between giving the correct answer and providing the right solution. These two desired outcomes, correct answer and right solution, are seldom analogous in the business of people.

I've encountered many an HR professional who can clearly and confidently explain 'what' HR does in great detail, but when challenged as to 'why' HR does those things, or does them in that way, the answers are often suddenly somewhat inadequate, less clear and less confident. This suggests to me that, when delivering solutions into the business, we can fall into the trap of thinking that doing the 'what' competently is sufficient for us to justify our existence in and of itself, without any real requirement for explaining *why* those things are necessary, let alone why they may be 'good' or 'value add'.

This means that the building blocks required to achieve 'knowing HR' are both 'what' HR does and 'why' HR does those 'whats'. Unpacking 'how' we do those 'whats' is our destination on this journey together. We will explore these 'hows' in each chapter throughout this book.

Knowing the 'what' and being the 'how'

This is the point at which I need to write my second introduction (or at least to remind us of the first). This book is not written to expound the 'what' of that which we or the wider-HR department should be doing, as there are plenty of curricula, sound textbooks and common practice which extensively cover that subject. I do not plan to bore you here with an exhaustive list of HR functions.

Suffice to say when I refer to HR practice, HR generalist or HR in terms of product or function, I mean that we can be expected to know something about topics pertaining broadly to the functions of: employee relations; industrial relations; employment law; HR policy; reward and benefits; recruitment; HR systems and processes; organizational design; organizational development; learning; talent management; well-being; and diversity and inclusion. Hopefully this broad range of HR subjects illustrates why it is described as 'being a generalist'.

THE SOMETIMES-STRANGE TALE OF ORGANIZATIONAL DEVELOPMENT AND HUMAN RESOURCES

I have listed organizational development (OD) as a core function of human resources. This may be a controversial point to some, and I hope not to have upset OD professionals by bundling them in with the overall offerings of the HR function. I believe organizational development interventions are most effective when presented to the business through the medium of the HR business partner, as part of the overall HR offering. This is the recipe for delivery of successful organizational design interventions.

Unhelpfully, I have encountered an incomprehensible trend of structuring an organizational development function outside of the HR function as if it is some sort of alien force sent to take over the world (or at least to conquer the HR function). This unusual practice includes the head of OD (or equivalent role) reporting to someone other than an HR director. This set up seems very strange to me and creates numerous amounts of practical and cross-functional issues that make it much more difficult for an organization to create and follow a coherent people agenda.

Structures alone are by no means an effective method of fixing a problem, but a flawed structure can create problems that were not there before.

Under the centres of expertise model (COE), many HR functions will employ specialists in each of the functions listed. It is worth noting that almost every HR department, no matter the size, will seek to provide all these services to their people. Our HR departments really are doing a lot for us.

These subjects are, for the purposes of 'knowing HR', the 'what' of HR practice and service offerings. The HR business partner is the mechanism for 'how' these specialist subjects are translated and delivered within a business.

I mean that in the broadest possible sense. I understand of course many people would put forward that systems, processes and subject-matter-expert(s)-designers make up the lion's share of 'how' these subjects are delivered within businesses. I would counter by suggesting, in a broad sense, that humans will have a natural reluctance to engage with these fantastic systems and processes without a trusted advocate. This well-understood and natural human trait of resistance to change creates the requirement for a skilled intermediary who can traverse the vagaries of HR specialisms and translate them for different business leaders. The common HR operating models often reflect this struggle between experts and HR business partners; for our purposes I will proceed on the basis that both are required. Let the debate rage on!

Those who take up HR business partner roles are often sourced from those who already have a 'generalist' HR background and knowledge broadly covering the range of functions I have listed, so that they may be able to operate on behalf of the HR function at large.

However, historically many generalists have fallen short in the role because their knowledge and experience are too narrow. In these cases where knowledge is too narrow, I have found that individuals' generalist knowledge is limited to employee relations, recruitment, policy, employment law and their corresponding systems and processes (let's refer to these individuals as the 'RERPELS' – Recruitment Employee Relations Policy Employment Law and Systems).

RERPELS are unlikely, in my view, to be able to fulfill my definition of 'competent' generalists. Much, much, more knowledge is required to perform. This point may upset some people, but my intention is always to build up and not tear down. Outrage is often the first step on the journey of change. Realization is the second.

I'm speaking to this specifically because I was originally a RERPELS, but fortunately I did not stay that way. Therefore, I know firsthand the importance of broadening out the knowledge of a generalist. Of course, it is quite hard, if not practically impossible, to be expert in each and every one of the specialist subjects above and so inevitably generalists will have differing depths of knowledge on each function based on their previous experience.

What the 'competent' generalist must remember (and usually has the benefit of), is that we are not actually required to be expert in specialisms. Let alone to be expert in this number of specialisms.

As mentioned earlier, within larger organizations there will be subject matter experts in some or all of the specialist subjects listed above, and the presence of those experts in itself dictates the business's desire for activity in those areas. However, on this point, it is unfortunate that oftentimes job titles, and not coherent strategy, drive activity. We cannot underestimate the power of coherent strategy within our businesses to inform what we do.

This is where the role of an HR business partner within HR is quite different to everyone else within the HR function. The people-expert-business-partner is required to know what every role within HR does, exactly how it impacts the business and why those functions are necessary.

Subject-matter-experts within HR can rely on being expert in what they do without necessarily having deep knowledge of what everyone else within the function does. This is the role of the HR business partner. It is we who must translate all these specialisms for, and on behalf of, an unwitting business. We will have to explain the offerings of the HR function and answer the inevitable questions on solutions that were occasionally generated without regard to the needs of specific business functions (or to phrase it in the positive, solutions) that were generated for the organization at large and not tailored for individual needs. Many ineffective, impractical, irrelevant or untranslatable schemes and solutions have been developed in detail behind closed doors without any reference to anyone or anything besides a textbook. Theory must usually be applied practically and not literally,

FIGURE 1.1   The HR business partner blended balance

SOURCE Glenn Templeman (2021)

and the HR business partner offers that insight to how something will work in practice. Moreover, we often must knit together a myriad of HR offerings into one presentable whole package of coherent services for business leaders.

The role is unique within the HR function in this regard. We must face inwards and outwards simultaneously, perfectly balancing and blending the wants and needs of both HR and the business in the process. This blended balance is where we develop solutions that effectively deliver the HR agenda and are also tailored to meet the individual business area needs. Figure 1.1 shows that the solutions we create as HR business partners must be comprised of both the HR function's own agenda and offering, as well as individual business area requirements. Effective solutions are blended together by HR business partners in this white space between the HR offerings and the business requirements.

In terms of the type of person who is capable to become 'competent' in this role, I am considering this point from a purist's perspective and imagining that any HR generalist with a weighting in one, or any, of these HR specialisms could take on the role of an HR business partner. Whereas most commonly we seem to have risen from the position of generalist HR advisors as opposed to from roles within learning and development, organizational development etc.

Typically, this well-traversed career path is defined by being experts in employee relations, policy, employment law and their corresponding systems and processes (RERPELS). As we have established, 'knowing HR', or 'knowing the what', is far broader than this. I suspect that organizations with the highest-performing HR business partner teams contain individuals whose backgrounds are more diverse than the RERPELS of old. Hopefully this is a legacy issue that we will shake off as time goes on.

HR for life

We should keep in sharp focus why this primary point of 'knowing HR' is indeed primary and most important for us to be successful. It is because however good we are, however trusted we become, however much value we add and contribute to the strategic direction and delivery of the business areas we serve, when they see us coming they will always think, 'Here is [fill in your name] from HR', and that is a good thing.

An important nuance here – sometimes they will see us coming and think, 'Here is [fill in your name] my HR business partner', but never will they think, 'Here is [fill in your name] my partner with whom I'm in business'. The order of the words is important as the title has run away with itself a little over the years. This is a subtle but important difference. I cannot overstate the point that however good we are, and however many fanciful titles we give ourselves, we should still behave as a support service. As Abraham Lincoln is purported to have once said, 'How many legs does a dog have if you call his tail a leg? Four. Calling a tail a leg doesn't make it a leg.'

This is a good thing, because our job is HR. As obvious as this may sound (it is in the business partner title after all), it is easy to make this mistake when we are an appreciated part of the business area team and have our fingers in every aspect of the business. Under these circumstances it is easy to get carried away and somehow see ourselves as something greater than their HR representative.

The business needs their HR business partner to help them with many things but first, always first, they need us to translate their HR department for them, and to do that we must first know 'everything' about HR: from the overarching purpose and function of the department down to everything it does, how it goes about doing it and why it is done in that way.

So, to begin with, if we do not know everything about HR we are going to mess this up, which will cause damage to our reputation and the reputation of the HR function. We cannot have people-experts who do not know what everyone in HR does and why they do it. Of course, some messing up is permitted, it is a common factor of being human after all, as none of us are perfect.

An important fundamental attribute to consider here is the importance of perception. In the people game, perception really is king. Even when we find ourselves wildly out of control, confused or lost, our people still have the intrinsic need to trust us. They need to trust what we say and think and trust the advice that we give.

To protect this earnt trust, we must first cultivate amongst others a perception of ourselves that allows them to place their trust in us and our role. We must continue to act in a way that is conducive to maintaining this built trust. It is beholden upon us to consider how we will be perceived with every piece of advice we give and every decision we make.

That said, I find that how we are perceived is entirely within our own control. Hopefully you have the freedom of choice to govern how you conduct yourself at work. Careful thought should be given to how we wish to be perceived, and how that perception will help to cultivate the required trust that will ultimately give us the bandwidth to operate the full facets of the people-expert-business-partner role. This is a key component in being a people-expert.

This is an intentionally circular point. If we know enough about people to control how we wish to be perceived by them, then we must be an expert in people, and to be a people-expert we must be able to master the perception challenge.

The seed of credibility

Knowing 'everything' about HR is the seed of credibility; credibility as a business partner must be seeded in something and for us that seed is our comprehensive knowledge of HR, what, how and why. Without this primary thing we risk becoming corporate company representatives with some half-baked ideas enforcing 'the way things are done here'. I can only say I hope this does not sound at all familiar to you, although unfortunately I expect it is something most of us have experienced at some point.

There are many dangers in seeding our credibility in something other than our knowledge of HR, whether that be in a past success, a particular relationship (watch out for this one!) or knowledge of a business area. These things are important, and we will come to them, but for anything to replace knowledge of HR as the seed of credibility is a misalignment or dislocation that will ultimately cause damage. The definition of a seed is: 'the unit of reproduction of a flowering plant, capable of developing into another such plant' (Oxford Languages, 2021). Seeds do not grow different plants to the seed, therefore we should be very careful in what we choose to seed ourselves.

Knowing HR, and therefore being able to credibly deliver on an HR-designed people agenda for business areas, is the first half of the delicate HR business partner archetype.

Summary

Knowing HR is essential to being a competent HR business partner. We achieve this by understanding everything HR does, both what we do and why we do it. We use this knowledge of HR to translate our services and offerings to the business, ensuring HR initiatives are designed and delivered successfully. Our role is to intimately understand the 'what' and the 'why' of HR so that we can be the 'how' to the organization. We maintain our roots in HR so that we can effectively bridge the gap between HR and the business. We use this comprehensive knowledge of HR as the basis of our credibility with the business and its leaders. Next, let's explore the corresponding second part of the foundational structure: knowing the business.

Reference

Oxford Languages (2021) Seed, *Oxford English Dictionary*, Oxford University Press

02

Knowing the business

The HR business partner archetype

I'm attempting to unpack the HR business partner role in a bottom-up way, so that if you are new to HR or considering a career in HR, you can take these chapters and apply them sequentially in order to progress your career and be successful in delivering business outcomes through people. This order is generally reflective of the way we learn these things working in the HR profession, and our intentional order here is not only sequential or chronological, we will find that it is also a mostly organic progression. I cannot think of any circumstances where one is required to perform a strategic HR role without first having the baseline knowledge of HR.

So, to be successful, whilst we are developing a competent level of knowledge in HR, as set out in Chapter 1, we then also need to develop this same level of knowledge of the business. Think of it as a traditional set of weighing scales, the kind held by blindfolded lady justice outside a court of law: on the one side is the knowledge of HR and on the other the knowledge of the business. The two should balance, with the HR knowledge on one side and the knowledge of the business on the other.

This balancing of knowledge is the HR business partner archetype and is required for us to be effective in our role. It is unique within the plethora of HR roles to only the HR business partner. The knowledge of the business is the second half of this delicate archetype.

This balancing act is essential because a tip towards either side always creates some kind of friction or anxiety on the opposite side. This condition has been so prevalent that we have even employed a phrase to describe those who tip this balance too far towards the business. Unfortunately, this is the reason we are all familiar with the phrase 'going native' in the HR profession. I will address this point in more detail later in this chapter.

No role left unturned

I really hate interviewing. I used to love it, but then I ended up doing huge volumes of interviews in my early career and it quickly became tedious and repetitive. There must be a happy medium where we can maintain our interviewing sharpness and people insights without having to do huge volumes and burn out on the whole concept as an assessment method. I do not profess to know what that happy medium is, however.

After many years of this, the request to 'support with interviews' is entirely groan-inducing followed by careful diary manipulation to give the appearance of non-availability.

DIARY DANCER

Don't tell me you haven't done this. Leaving that cancelled 3-hour meeting in the diary just so that something else doesn't get booked in its place and you can instead do some actual 'work'. Sending opaque smoke signals to those that would dare to use a scheduling assistant to send a meeting request. There are some people who have completely mastered this art – they have become full-blown diary wizards and there really is no way to tell what they are doing when, let alone where they might be on any given day! These individuals are impervious to meeting requests. Although I often find this practice quite amusing it is also very annoying.

Whilst we are on the subject, I have to take the opportunity to vent my spleen against the practice of blocking out diaries for the completion of 'tasks'. Fair enough if it is only every now and then for the completion of a significant time-bound task, but the increasingly common practice of filling most of the diary for most of each week with reoccurring instances of tasks (and not meetings) must stop. Diaries are for meetings not tasks.

If we cannot cope because all our time is taken up with meetings, skip ahead to Chapter 11 for the answers. You are very welcome.

However, I have been reminded again of the benefit of interviewing – it is often the most efficient way of learning what a business unit does and how the role we are interviewing for contributes to the overall business.

Interviewing has at least two key obvious benefits: 1) we gain an intimate understanding of the role way beyond the words written on the page of the job description; and 2) we get to meet a range of people who may be suitable to undertake the role and listen to them tell us all about the things they have done previously that are relevant to the performance of this role.

It is as if the whole process is designed, not to assess the best candidate, but as a method of market research into the role and the best-practice approach to its performance, as if it is a method for a layperson third-party to understand the role in a more intimate way. No wonder that when used in isolation the interview does not always yield great people for the performance of the role.

This medium of market research is important in achieving the knowledge of the business that we seek. We will need to do plenty of this sort of research if we are to grow in our knowledge of the business we serve. However, I must provide an instant caveat here, our role is clearly not to conduct interviews ad infinitum. For our purposes it is a tool to be used tactically for learning. This tool is particularly useful to us when joining a new organization or when switching within the business to partner a new or different business area. We should relieve ourselves from any feelings of moral obligation to always say 'yes' to requests to sit on interview panels.

In my view, the golden rule here is that the HR business partner should know what *every* role within our business areas does. Every role. For me this is a basic requirement to be successful in our role. We cannot do our jobs effectively unless we understand what everyone else's job is.

I am not exaggerating for effect (which I am prone to do by the way), knowing what each role does is a key component building block that we must achieve. This knowledge is a key step towards truly knowing the business.

If we can have an in-depth understanding of all the roles within a business area, and how those roles interact with each other to perform the business function, it will give us a wealth of knowledge when dealing with the full spectrum of people matters. It provides us with a platform to develop our business knowledge from, whilst also helping to inform everyday decisions, and solutions to novel problems. Having this knowledge platform enables us to be informed business advisors, as opposed to advisors on matters of HR policy. This is an essential and important distinction.

Fundamentally, this is one of the key and vital differences between the HR business partner role and the HR subject matter expert roles that I started to unpack in the previous chapter.

Therefore, knowing all the roles and what they do is part of the prerequisite specialist knowledge, unique to the role of HR. In Chapter 1 we have already explored the functions of the HR business partner generalist and the background that HR business partners often have – RERPELS. Others within the HR function can be relied upon for deep technical expertise, and we should be relied upon for deep knowledge of our respective business areas.

The oft-missed subtlety within our profession is that the HR business partner *is* the business area people subject matter expert. This might be an under-appreciated or overlooked point. In life we tend to box 'expertise' into things that it is possible to gain a qualification in. However, it is clear to me that we are the subject matter experts on the people and roles within our business areas, despite the lack of available academic qualification in this subject. This expertise makes up a good deal of the fuel driving the vehicle in the successful roll out of HR initiatives.

This subject matter expertise can be deployed both into the business area directly, to tailor people solutions to fit the business, and also back into HR to translate and interpret what the business wants and needs. We facilitate this circular feedback loop, constantly translating and advocating the motivations and details of each side's requirements. Explaining the business to the HR function and the HR function to the business. This is the essence of our role. It goes both ways and we are required to straddle both worlds simultaneously and seamlessly.

This circular feedback loop is set out in Figure 2.1, which also shows the internal and external factors that we must incorporate into

FIGURE 2.1   The HR business partner paradigm

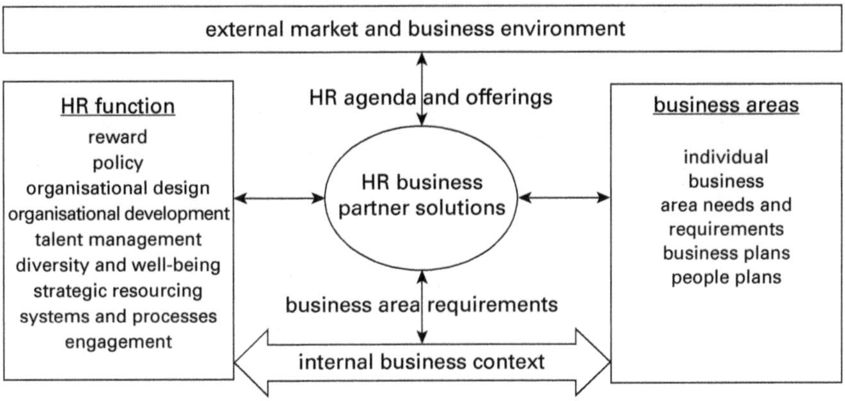

SOURCE Glenn Templeman (2014)

our solutions and outcomes. Figure 2.1 is a direct augmentation of Figure 1.1, and shows the entire picture that we must consume to create effective solutions.

The arrows demonstrate the factors within which the business partner is required to work, connecting the external market environment to the internal business context, whilst delivering appropriate HR agenda and offerings that take into account the business area requirements.

The diagram depicts the strategic positioner and influencing nature of the HR business partner to enable development and delivery of HR solutions that are fit for the business, the market and the organizational context.

Problems will start to occur when this perfect straddling balance is not simultaneous and seamless. We will quickly lose credibility with either side if we are perceived as too strongly or too often representing the views of one side over the other.

The people currency

Knowing all the roles within a business area leads us on to a natural progression: knowing all the people. This may sound like an improbable task, but anyone who has worked within an HR function for a while will know that we quickly get to recognize most of the names within a business area or perhaps an entire organization, depending on the size.

In my experience I would say that if you work within an organization for a couple of years it is possible to recognize more than 1000 names on a page, spreadsheet or intranet phonebook. If you have worked in an organization for much longer then we might find that 'recognition number' rises above 2000 and perhaps much higher for some. When considering this point, I personally thought that on one occasion my own 'recognition number' may have been over 3000 names.

I have no detailed scientific or mathematic research to underpin this idea, this 'recognition number' theory is purely based on my own experience. I suspect the 'recognition number' is probably higher if you are an introvert or have a natural interest in people. I've made an underlying assumption throughout that I am talking to a people group who do have a high level of interest in people!

Understanding all the roles within a business and how they interact seems a somewhat logical requirement for us in our quest to know the business. However, when it comes to knowing all the people, some might question why this is an important or essential component of being an HR business partner. The fundamental reason being, because again, we are the people subject matter expert and people are the currency in which we trade our value. The roles are one thing, but we are not role-expert-advisers, we are *people*-expert-advisers. The individual people bring the roles to life, and seldom do two people perform the same role the same way. We are not robots. There is still value in being human and it is for us to unlock and nurture this value for the business.

This knowledge can be used in lots of different ways, two of which I will address in the following sections, but the key point to understand is that knowing HR and then knowing the business, its roles and its people, are all key building blocks to successfully harnessing and influencing the whole organization to move in the direction of achieving its goals.

Smoothing the path

Let us step further back from this point briefly and consider it in practice. If we have a person who has formed a strong and trusted relationship with a director and their respective leadership team, *and* this person is an advocate for the organization's own internal professional people department, *and* is a knowledgeable authority on the subject and function of HR, *and* also has a developed and intimate understanding of: 1) the business area function(s); 2) all of the roles within the business area; and 3) all of the people currently employed within that business – then this person will surely have placed themselves on solid ground from which to build.

Almost anything can be built from a platform such as this, but for our purposes it will be used initially to build trust, confidence and credibility in ourselves. This may sound selfish, subversive and self-serving, but ours is a relationships business, people are not necessarily a meritorious business. Trust must be earned and built, credibility is not measured out and gifted based on roles or seniority.

It is my view, and I think also the view of many other HR professionals and HR business partners, that the example described above is the prevailing structure for the archetypal HR business partner. This is the platform from which we must add everything else, and from which the overarching HR function will have to rely upon for the delivery of successful people initiatives.

The HR function is reliant upon, and expectant that, we will deliver a smooth path into the respective business areas to enable the HR function at large to deliver on what it has promised to do.

This 'making a smooth path' is the kind of base-level staple use of the hard work that we all put in to 'knowing HR' and 'knowing the business'. It is a very important use, and, as I said previously, it makes the whole HR function successful when the team is able to do what it said it would. Many HR promises are fulfilled via the pre-existing relationships of HR business partners.

WHOSE RELATIONSHIP IS IT ANYWAY?

In the delivery of important HR initiatives, a relationship tug-o-war can occasionally ensue between the HR business partner and the HR subject matter expert responsible for the initiative. Suffice to say, from our perspective some HR subject matter experts may disagree to some extent with the HR business partner being cast in the role of 'promise-fulfiller'.

It is very useful for HR subject matter experts to develop great relationships with people out in the business areas. However, that is not the primary function of the subject matter expert's role. Instead, the primary function is to be a deep expert in a specific HR specialism. It is the HR business partner who has the responsibility of facilitating the link between HR and the business to enable HR initiatives to be delivered (amongst other things). The HR subject matter expert needs their HR business partner to be strong so that they too can be strong.

So, the first way in which we use this knowledge of the business to enable the organization to achieve its goals is to facilitate the HR function to deliver on achieving its own goals. This is important because the people function has its own strategy and aims designed upon the organization's overarching ambitions and values.

The second way in which we harness the knowledge of the business to enable the organization to achieve its goals is by supporting the respective business areas it serves to organize and lead its people successfully, in line with business area goals. These are also important as they cumulatively contribute to the prosperity of the business at large.

Harnessing the knowledge of the business can take many forms and is an activity that takes place every day, applied in all that we think, say and do, on a micro and macro level. At a macro level this knowledge could be applied to the successful delivery of a comprehensive organizational design and corresponding restructure. At the micro level the knowledge is applied in a thousand corridor conversations that help to nudge and point people in the right direction. Suffice to say there are a million other uses in-between, all of which contribute to supporting business areas in the delivery of their local area goals and objectives.

Predicting the future

One point that is worthy of particular attention here, however, is the ability of the people-expert with knowledge of the business to exercise the gift of foresight. This foresight is offered, we must remember, from the position of an individual who is an expert in the professional field of people, has a deep understanding of the business and also has developed knowledge of all of the people within that business. These three components combined ought to create something that is greater than the sum of its parts. That something, I believe, is foresight.

I must choose my words carefully here because when we speak of people who can predict the future, we quickly stray into the space of 'added value', which is reserved for Chapter 3. Nevertheless, I will deal with applied foresight briefly here as it is a direct and natural by-product of knowing the business.

In simple terms here, if we know everything about HR, the business and all the people in the business, and we purport to be an 'expert' in the subject of people, then surely that means we will be able to apply that knowledge to predict how people will respond in given situations, and to decipher what they will or won't do next. It sounds a little seditious, but this is really very valuable knowledge to any leader or business function. Any business leader would value a trustworthy and reliable method of predicting how their people will react to different scenarios or telling what their people may do or think in each scenario. Experienced HR business partners know this of course, we are doing it every day.

In organizations with a well-developed HR business partnering function you might hear about those who are said to 'have their fingers on the pulse' or be at the 'heartbeat' of the business. This is indeed a common feature that we should be working to attain. So, I must ask, what is the point of having our fingers on the pulse if we do not use it to deduce the resting heartrate? Assessing the pulse and deducing the heartrate are the beginnings of using what we know to predict what is likely to happen next.

Forward-thinking leadership teams will expect this of us, and it often comes in the form of a simple question, 'What do you think about this?', which is loaded with expectation in this area of foresight. What really is being asked is, 'Based on your knowledge, 1) can we do this, and 2) how will our people respond if we do?'

This type of question asked consistently, and persistently, to HR business partners means that it really is beholden upon us to become somewhat competent in the area of applied foresight. To qualify what I mean by 'somewhat competent' in this business of predicting the future, I feel that we must get it mostly right between 70–80 per cent of the time. This is of course a feeling judgement, not a binary percentage target to be accurately calculated. I think this level of accuracy is sufficient to continue building credibility and trust across leadership teams and peers.

We must see the people problems before they arise; we must predict the people-related challenges so that they can be mitigated or avoided as appropriate.

Whose side are you on?

I must end this section on 'knowing the business' with a warning, even though it may be a warning familiar to most of us. That oh-so-familiar warning about getting too close to the business: going native.

I think HR business partners 'going native' occurs a lot less often than we tend to talk about it happening in the world of HR. I suppose in its simplest form it is based on an idea that the business and HR are eternally set against each other and that there are people who can move from one side to the other, for which we designate them as having 'gone native'. Personally, I'm not sure this theory about sides is necessarily true and it is certainly not helpful for HR professionals to think in this way. Hopefully, with this thought in mind and our own prior experience, we have already started to debunk this as erroneous and remove it from our thinking. In our own defence, I do think this idea can often be triggered by the business leader promoting the 'I'm human so I know about people' mantra that I explained in the Introduction.

My warning would simply be this: do not focus so hard on this principle of knowing the business that we forget how we came to be embedded in that business in the first place. As mentioned in Chapter 1, our primary function is to be HR experts, not business experts.

As HR business partners we can easily avoid the 'going native' trap by regularly assessing our relationships and feelings towards our own HR function. A telltale sign can often be saying things like 'I'll talk to HR' or 'it's HR's error'. Our words will give away how we really see ourselves. How we see the HR function impacts upon how we see ourselves within the organization. Mixing up this perception often causes or indicates that we have gone, or are going, native.

As a side point here, if this situation becomes acute and you are accused of declaring UDI (universal declaration of independence), as I have been myself in the dim and distant past, you are definitely off course and you can expect that something significant of some sort is likely to happen in resolution! Something to be avoided in our career highlights!

It seems to me that entire books could be written on this principle of why HR business partners should know the business, and perhaps this was the motivation behind the Ulrich concept of business part-nering and the reason the role was invented. I hope that here I have done enough to at least build an initial framework of thought upon which further reflection, creativity and innovation can be built.

The HR business partner cannot operate one-handed with only the knowledge of HR, we must also build this business knowledge – to think otherwise is, in my view, a fundamental misunderstanding, or an unmerited application of arrogance!

Summary

In summary, knowing the business is the counterweight with which we balance our knowledge of HR. We can begin to develop this busi-ness knowledge through the day-to-day performance of our roles. We do this by getting to understand every role within a business area, and subsequently by also getting to know as many of the people performing those roles as possible. We can then harness this knowledge of the business, its roles and its people to establish our own credibility and develop trust as a partner of the business. Ultimately, we harness this business knowledge to enable the organization to meet its business and people goals. Then, as an established expert of HR with comprehensive knowledge of the business, we can start to predict how people will respond and react, pre-empting people-related issues before they occur. Finally, we must remember from whence we came and ensure we stay on the right side of our namesake team, striking the ultimate balance between HR and business needs.

Next, we will explore the final part of our short but comprehensive foundational structure – adding value.

03

Adding value

A cord of three strands

Our foundational structure is tripartite by design and therefore our two-sided HR business partner archetype set out in Chapter 2 is not complete without being underpinned by this third strand of adding value. This final piece of the foundational structure completes our three-pronged basis for success as HR business partners. As depicted in Figure 3.1, each strand is essential and holds up the other strands to ensure the foundation is comprehensive and creates a strong footing for the long journey ahead.

It is therefore essential that we address this principle of 'adding value' third, as only the principles of 'knowing HR' and 'knowing the business' should come before adding value. The order of these three is significant and not to be overlooked. Knowing HR, knowing the business and adding value is our essential foundation, and is the platform from which everything else will be added. These three things are required in this order when seeking to build and maintain a sustainable trust and credibility. This is the structural framework from which we can add every other skill that we must master. Once we know the things that are most important to know (HR and the business), we must then consider how best to apply the knowledge we have mastered so that we add value.

If any one of these three strands are missing from our foundational structure, we will become lopsided, insufficient or ineffective in our roles. Imagine being an HR business partner without the knowledge

FIGURE 3.1   The foundational structure

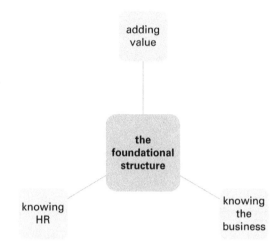

SOURCE Glenn Templeman (2020)

of HR or without gaining any local area business knowledge. The same is true if we have both those things without adding value over and above what the HR function could have done without us.

An HR business partner without all three parts of the foundational structure will not be able to fulfill the full potential of the role. In order to hit the target, we must know what we are aiming for, and ensure we use the very important tools required for success.

If we have this tripartite foundational structure at the root of our business partnering offering, then I believe we are setting ourselves up for success. This is the basic formula for producing people-expert business-transforming HR business partners.

Everyday value

Most people have enough self-awareness to know whether their presence is likely 'to add' anything to a meeting or a conversation. Saying, 'I'm not sure if I will add anything by being there', is a simple but honest turn of phrase that we hear often, most commonly used in the pursuit of prioritization. No one desires to be involved in something if it is not useful for them to do so – it may equate to a waste of their time if they won't be able to make meaningful contributions. This is a good train of thought for us to employ: if we cannot add anything then maybe we do not need to be involved, except where there are opportunities for learning or gleaning relevant information. This is true of the general idea of being able to 'add' or contribute to activities in the workplace, but subtly different to our concept of adding value.

In our roles we should consider adding value as a perpetual state of being. Conversely to not being able to add anything, we should aim to always be able to add value to the businesses we serve. The combination of knowing HR and knowing the business must lead us to a place of harnessing that delicate knowledge balance to create added value for our businesses. It is not enough for us to just deliver the initiatives of the wider HR function and think that alone equates to adding value in our roles. It is imperative upon us to connect the dots between our knowledge of people practice and our developing knowledge of the business to seek out opportunities to add value way beyond the sum of these parts.

The question of 'adding value' is not a new or novel idea for the HR community, it has been with us for as long as I can remember. It has become an enduring topic and so it should remain. I am encouraged, when I look back upon my career, that HR functions seem to have progressed from never considering whether we were adding value, to a juxtaposed present day where adding value appears to be engrained in our collective psyche. It is a given that we are focused on adding value, not just as HR business partners, but as the whole HR function.

So, having established the essential nature of a service underpinned by adding value, at this point I must pose the provocative question: if this thought is somehow engrained in our collective and individual psyches, why do we so often falter in understanding what adding value really looks like? In addition to this question, why do we sometimes struggle to clearly demonstrate how we add value to a business?

I'm not seeking here to polarize anyone by asking these questions, but I am instead aiming to test our understanding and stimulate thought on this essential question of how we add value.

What or where?

Hopefully, by now we are all asking ourselves the same question: what exactly is value-add activity? How can we quantify it, and can we create a clear and coherent list of these value-add activities for the HR business partner so that we can get on with doing those value-add tasks? Unfortunately, I think those are the wrong questions and that approach would be far too reductive in the pursuit of achieving real value. Only you will be able to determine exactly what added value looks like to the business areas you serve, based on your balanced and combined knowledge of HR and the business. However, I can show you *where* added value usually occurs.

There is usually a natural gap between the organization-wide offerings and initiatives of the HR function and the individual wants

FIGURE 3.2   The HR business partner value-add gap

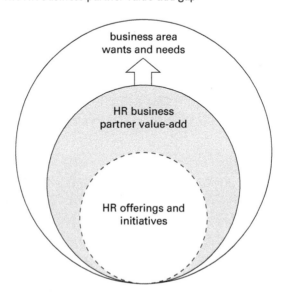

SOURCE Glenn Templeman (2021)

and needs of diverse business areas in respect of their people. This is the gap that the HR business partner bridges positionally but, also in this case, as a difference maker in the pursuit of realizing value in people practice, over and above what the HR function at large can offer. Figure 3.2 shows this gap which often exists and is required to be filled by the HR business partner in pursuing tailored business solutions. Note that the dotted line indicates that HR business partnering is an HR offering in itself.

Understanding where we fit in the equation between HR and the business enables us to know where and when we add value, which in turn I hope provides for you a clear indication of *how* you can add value in your day-to-day operation of the HR business partner role. Applying our well-developed knowledge base of HR and the business to an understanding of where we add value and how, should provide easy answers to the question of *what* value-add activity looks like.

Two sides of the same coin

In order that we can properly target real value-add activity it is also useful to have an appreciation of that which is not value-add activity. For quite some time now we in HR have been asking ourselves how we define added value in our work. Despite our focus on adding value, I believe we sometimes struggle with this question of how to define 'value-add work'. It seems to me that the reason for this is that we often lack a simple and clear formula for conversely determining that which is *not* 'value-add work'.

If you have only ever been shown what to do, instead of having been able to define for yourself *how* an outcome is achieved, then flicking a switch in your mind to suddenly define the creation of value may be a difficult task. In this case, perhaps we should instead be turning our immediate attention to that which we can see is not adding value. If we tackle the problem by first identifying the activities that do not add value and seek to remove them from our offerings, this will naturally lead us toward undertaking activity that *does* add value.

I find the question of how to add value often requires a degree of creative thinking. There are of course some creative people out there who have no trouble with the question of 'how to add value', but here I'm writing for the many who I see struggle with this question and for those who are at an early stage in their career and may be less familiar with this principle of adding value. The natural career progression of many HR business partners has meant that countless individuals have gone from processing transactional tasks, to advisory activity then quickly onto business partnering. This natural progression sometimes makes it hard for individuals to change their mindset at the same pace, from inputs and rules associated with transactional and advisory tasks, to the outcome-focused objectives required for business partnering.

Self-assessment

If I am correct in my observations that some of us are struggling with this concept of how we add value, then a potentially better question to ask, or a better angle of attack, is to consider the work we currently do and assess whether all of this current activity is adding value to the business.

This inflection point will be helpful to us in two ways: 1) it provides a simple alternative principle from which to consider the value-add question, with an opportunity to objectively assess that which is not adding value; and 2) most excitingly, it gives us the opportunity to assess our current work and actually get rid of some of it, on the basis that it does not add value at all, or that it does not add value for us to do it, and therefore the work would be better assigned somewhere else.

Incidentally I am a big fan of getting rid of work, it really is a very exciting prospect indeed. Whilst it is not worthy to be covered here in our principles, those that have worked with me closely know that it is a principle that I seek to exercise relentlessly throughout my working life, with the aim of benefiting everyone involved. Take a moment to ponder on this perhaps unusual point and think of it another way: we are always being asked to do more with less, so if that is our modern-day context then we must also learn to get rid of the less value-add work. I should be clear here that adding value is by no means an exercise in doing more things. I will address this point in more detail in Chapter 11.

Time and time again I observe the diligent HR business partner committing their precious time, energy and effort, to that which appears, in my view, to not add value. It is my view that this occurs not because these people are mad, bad or sad (although we are often at least one of these things!), but because we possess no clinical formula for determining that which does not add value. I do think that if we had such a formula then we could at the very least develop a greater self-awareness of how we are using our time. Ideally, however, understanding where we are not adding value would instead lead us to the ultimate destination of focusing our time and effort on value-add activity.

If past experience of well-meaning HR functions is anything to go by, thinking continuously about new and creative ways to add value seems to have the countereffect of adding no value at all. It is all too easy to become distracted, wrestling with the balance between the question of how to add value and our pre-existing day job, to notice that nothing or very little about our current work adds value.

In our roles as HR business partners we inevitably have a degree of autonomy to think and act. This means there is an extent to which we are allowed some independent thinking, and action, away from the collective HR offerings. This autonomy provides us with a great opportunity to reflect on our own activity within a business area and assess what is and is not adding value. If considering this question for ourselves, I believe it should be approached with a clean slate – the aim is not to augment our current workload with additional value-add activity. Instead, our aim should be to strip away that which does not add value and exclusively focus our time and attention on that which we believe adds value to the business. We must remember that adding value is not an exercise in doing more things.

The primary value-add test

Whilst I am hoping the concepts I have put forward are enabling us to be better informed when considering this question of added-value, I also wish to give us something simple and tangible we can take into the workplace and apply for ourselves. As I have already mentioned, my primary aim is to provide principles, not methods or exhaustive lists. However, this is one area where I feel it is useful to explain some of my personal methodology for practically assessing this question of adding value.

So, in the simplest of terms I suggest we could begin by applying this formula for determining that which does not add value: if a system, process, machine or set of well-ordered rules or guidelines could do this task, which I currently take time to do myself, then I am not adding value by doing it.

This first test is simply the 'Is there a better way to do this?' test. Systemization has been a fundamental feature of HR transformations in the 21st century. However, it can sometimes feel as though we still have a long way to go in pursuit of a systemized utopia and that there are many tasks that still require some sort of cumbersome or unnecessary human intervention. Therefore, this first test is still relevant and should help us to root out that which should have long-since been removed from our to-do lists.

It is worth a pause here for a targeted daydream about what of our current workload could essentially be codified in such a way to allow us to carve it away from the long list of things we spend our time on. Creating a list of all that we do and marking the activities that are not value-add, by the measure of this test, with a view to permanently striking them from our long list of responsibilities, then seeking to turn this into a reality, is something we should all be able to do immediately.

The secondary value-add test

Having considered whether there is a better way to do something, we can then turn our focus to the second value-add test. This secondary test may be particularly useful if we struggle with the application of the first test. The secondary test is a much broader test, which can be applied to the assessment of value-add within our current workload. It is a blunt instrument and will not necessarily yield as accurate a result as the first formula. Nevertheless, it is still a useful tool for managing both value and general workload and effectiveness, especially if used after the first formula has already been applied.

The second question to ask ourselves in the assessment of value-add activity is this: if someone else were to take on this activity today, how long would it take them to learn it and be able to perform the task to a competent level?

Now for the blunt instrument, if the answer to this question is anything less than six months, I would strongly suggest that it may not be value-add work for an HR business partner. Even six months may be too short a timeline and perhaps a much longer time period should be considered depending on the skills, experience and background of the person we had in mind when considering this question.

The test is a simple one: if anyone could come along and pick this up within six months or so and perform it without too much trouble, then it is likely that we should seek to shed this activity where possible – unless there is some specific value in us personally performing it. It is not a perfect test of course and sensible thought should be applied when considering this question. However, I find this is still an essential test for many of us, and one that often yields at least a handful of activities that we should not be doing ourselves.

This is not to diminish tasks that take less than six months to master. The performance of many key and important HR-related tasks can be learnt in six months or less. I would argue that the most important HR function of all, paying people, can usually be learnt in a much shorter timeframe than this. Often the differentiating factor here is between learning how to perform a task competently and gaining an authoritative knowledge of why we perform that task in that way. There is a good deal of difference between correctly processing the payroll for payment and understanding the whys and wherefores of all the myriad pay elements that make up the whole.

The key for us is not to mistake important, or even essential, for value-add. Our time must be ultimately focused on value-add activity.

There is a definite correlation between adding deep and lasting value to a business and the time it takes to learn to master this skill.

Looking to the future

Important and essential are tasks that we, and the HR function, are hopefully already doing today and must continue to do for the ongoing effective functioning of the organization. Value-add refers to the things that ensure the future survival, sustainability and required growth and development of the business. These are my definitions, which I hope you can easily take away and apply to your respective business areas and organizations. As I have indicated previously, setting out a list of value-add activity is not my aim. I am instead setting out principles, not exhaustive lists. In any case, about value-add, were I to set out a list of activities it would inevitably not apply equally to all of your individual circumstances and organizational traits.

When considering value-add activity for ourselves, our final reflection must be with one eye on the future. Considering our present offering and activity is important and essential. However, value-add activity is often waiting to be discovered in that which we are not doing today or not doing well enough today. Having an eye on the future, as we should always do, enables us to see what the business may need tomorrow. Having this forward-looking approach also prevents us from taking on activity that is not adding value, meaning that we never have the need to extricate ourselves from unnecessary tasks. This kind of pre-emptive strike can be a powerful tool to the HR business partner. Saying no to something when it first occurs is much easier than offloading activity we already have on our plate.

As HR business partners, we have a responsibility to primarily seek to focus our time and attention on that which adds value to our businesses. This will streamline our work and the clarity of our offerings to the businesses we serve. Successfully mastering this principle will magnify the experience and value of people within the workplace and the world of business. Answering the question of adding value is crucial for us in the pursuit, not only from the selfish point of creating interesting work for ourselves and the HR function, but ultimately and most importantly in defining the future of people and business at a universal level.

Summary

So, in summary, adding value is the third and final essential strand to our foundational structure. Everything else will be added to this strong foundation. Adding value is something we should be doing as part of the everyday performance of our roles. Moreover, we should think of it as a perpetual state of being. Most commonly, we will add value in the gaps that appear between the corporate offerings of the HR function and the discrete needs of individual business areas. This is where we add value to HR by refining new and existing initiatives, as well as adding value to the business by acting as a difference maker in the delivery of people practices. To ensure that we are truly undertaking value-add work it can be helpful to first seek to remove activities that we add no value by doing. This requires a critical self-assessment of our current activities and preferences, leveraging our own autonomy to identify and cut away that which does not add value. The first test of whether some activity is adding value is simply to ask, 'Is there a better way to do this?' The second test is more crude, less nuanced, and requires us to consider how quickly the task could be learnt by someone else. The principle being that if an activity could be mastered by another in a short period of time it is unlikely to be the type of value-add activity that we seek. Finally, when considering real value we must be looking to the future to assess what a business needs from its people-expert to be successful. This type of forward-looking assessment is the root of real value.

This brings us to the end of Part One of our journey. Next, I will introduce our people fundamentals, which are set out in Part Two.

PART TWO

The people fundamentals

Having established a foundational structure from which to build, we now turn our attention to the fundamentals of operating in the business of people. A kind of doctrine of HR.

In this part I have attempted to pull together all the absolutely essential themes that make up what is often referred to as the 'soft' side of the HR professional. Often these are the themes and concepts that make us human, and therefore a deeper knowledge and understanding of these is important for the people-expert.

These are all themes that exist intrinsically within HR functions and the people therein, but I find are rarely explicitly talked about.

These implicit themes of how to deal with people start to form the DNA of the HR business partner. They are a modus operandi which I feel has been lost but not forgotten in the evolution from old-fashioned tea and sympathy to modern business-focused human resources practice. Once again, these are a set of principles and traits, not an exhaustive list of methods.

Some of the concepts should at the very least be familiar, but I hope in this part to unpack and expound them in fresh ways so that we can grow in understanding of these ideas and learn to apply them in practice every day.

04

Always listen to people

The power of silence

Again, as with the start of Chapter 3, the order is important and intentional. I have tried to arrange my thoughts in order of those things that I consider to be most important in the building of success and credibility. Learning to arrange our thoughts is another key skill that we must master. If we do not know what we think then how will we know what to say? Such is the importance of listening that it must only follow after 'knowing HR', 'knowing the business' and 'adding value'. This is testament to the deep value of listening to others when trading in the currency of people.

A successful HR business partner will be truly predisposed to listening to others in all that they do. It is of utmost importance that as representatives of the HR function we make all and every effort to learn as much as we can about the business. This begins with a willingness, humility and ability to listen to all people, always. Not some of the people some of the time or the important-looking people all the time: all people, always. The aim here is to be generous with our listening, to always take the time to listen to people and respond positively to those who seek our counsel.

Fundamentally, the design of our role means that we must go out into a business that generally we do not contribute to directly, advise within specialisms that to begin with we know nothing about and sit at tables with people who know many things that we do not know. This is the underlying design of the HR business partner role and it provides the context for how we conduct ourselves and our people-related activities. We really cannot take it for granted that business leaders allow us to sit at their tables when initially we have such a limited knowledge of their technical specialisms.

This design requires not only a level of humility and acumen for us to be successful but at its most basic level, a willingness to truly listen, and to carefully apply that which is heard, will facilitate the required humility and help to build the necessary acumen. Listening is learning. Many an individual's career is limited only by how much they are willing to listen. In this context, 'listen' means listen, learn and apply what has been learnt through listening. If we are able to do all this by always listening, we will find ourselves in the minority who successfully embed listen, learn and apply into their everyday lives.

Generally, I think I am preaching to the choir regarding listening. I think a lot of us within HR have a reasonable grasp on various concepts and types of listening and how to deploy the techniques tactically and strategically, to our advantage and the advantage of others around us. Even so, we could not possibly proceed on our journey without dedicating time to considering why always listening is so important and how we can continue to cultivate this principle throughout our working lives. Always listening is the first building block we will add to our foundational structure as it is our critical enabler to facilitate mastering the role – nothing else can be learnt until we are listening.

Most of us will realize from our own experience that as soon as we open our mouth to talk, we are effectively saying, 'I know something, so it's worth listening to me over anyone else right now'. This implication is the natural product of an environment where only one person can be heard at a time (although perhaps this point applies even more so where everyone is shouting over each other!). Conversely, listening, and not speaking, implies that, 'my silence shows I'm listening to you and that you have something to say which is more worthwhile than what I would say right now'. We should be aware that by saying nothing, we are still saying something, even if it is only implied. There is a certain power that can be shared or expressed using silence in this way. This is a principle that we should champion in our roles and as HR professionals at large.

I do need to caveat this point by highlighting that we are talking about humans here and not machines. So, despite appearances levied by the use of silence, just as some people are never really saying anything worthwhile, it is also true that some people are never really listening! Contextual knowledge should be applied to this point – if you know an individual is prone to not listening then their silence should not be inferred to mean that on this occasion they are necessarily listening!

Delay, think, construct

We use listening as a tool in our everyday lives and in many ways throughout our working lives. We are familiar with a range of techniques associated with listening, particularly from our experience of job interviews or disciplinary meetings, and each of these listening techniques have different uses. We must be intentional in our use of listening, and to do that we need to know the key uses of listening for us to be successful in our roles.

I used to firmly believe, and perhaps still do, there were broadly speaking just two types of listening: 1) listening that benefits the person speaking; and 2) listening that benefits the person listening. This historical idea was borne from experiencing a large quantity of casework where I discovered listening was often more beneficial to the speaker than to the listener – people who feel they have been heard and had an opportunity to vent their spleen are always happier after they have finished speaking than they were before they started to speak. In that way, both types of listening will have some benefit to the listener!

During a conversation or meeting, solely thinking about what we are going to say next is not a form of listening. It is hard to listen constructively if we are only thinking of what we will say in response. That said, the first use of listening for us, I believe, is a purely tactical one: delay; think; construct. The conundrum we face in conversational arenas is to construct an accurate and comprehensive response quickly, without allowing our thinking to block out our listening.

- Delay – continuing to listen allows us more time to think, without thinking precluding our listening.
- Think – using listening to encourage someone to further expound a point, or to repeat themselves again, gives us an opportunity.

In practical terms, 'delay' and 'think' can be achieved by asking short prompt questions, such as:

- 'Can you go into more detail on that?'
- 'Can you explain your thinking on that?'
- 'Tell me more about that.'

This is by no means an exhaustive list of prompt questions, but I hope it gives you an idea of what could be used!

- Construct – as the speaker summarizes and likely repeats themselves using different words but not saying anything new, and we continue to offer listening, we can start to build a deeper understanding of the issues and piece together a suitable and comprehensive answer.

For those of us familiar with the HR business partner role, this very tactical deployment of listening is often learned and honed through undertaking, sometimes painful, volumes of casework but it serves us well later in the journey when listening to the latest serials of directors and other organizational authorities.

Listening to see

The second use of listening for us must be for the purposes of growth and learning. 'Knowing the business' is our second principle but thinking we know it completely is a failure of overconfidence or, perhaps more commonly, overfamiliarity. Unless it is a very simple business it is unlikely that we can be an expert in our first discipline, HR, and also be a deep expert in the specialist business of our current employer. We tend to think we understand that which we see all the time because, to save ourselves time and energy, we have created internal mental shortcuts for ease of processing the things we see, hear and talk about within a business area. Unfortunately, shortcuts are all they are, and there is no substitute for deep and thorough knowledge – silence is a useful tool, but it only gets us so far. We will always have something new to learn when it comes to knowing the business, and always listening is the fuel in our learning tank.

A commitment to always listening in this context will reap rewards that pay us back many times over. Personally, I struggle to see the downsides of being a generous listener, provided it is well managed and in keeping with the other principles set out in this book. Our willingness to always listen and grow in our knowledge of the business is integral to building trust, confidence and key relationships. Let us remember that business leaders are actively looking for advocates and supporters of their cause. Many business leaders will find themselves in a constant battle for survival where only war-footings will do. This can create a divisive atmosphere, but it also offers us the open-door opportunity to closely align ourselves with our business areas. This does of course mean that from time to time we will be required to get in the proverbial trench with those business leaders with whom we have aligned ourselves. Through listening we are seeking to become an advocate for the business (we are by default already an advocate for HR). The opportunities provided by pressure, conflict or hostilities are just one way our listening habit can be used to unlock and develop essential relationships with business leaders.

These positions on the local business area battlefield cannot be located or well understood by a layperson unless they are committed to listening in this context. As described earlier in this chapter, listening to benefit only oneself is not sufficient to develop the necessary understanding required to earn a 'seat at the table'. Many are gifted a seat at the leadership team table these days, but too few go on to earn it or validate the original gifting. The assumption here is, if we have a seat then we have a voice. Few of us can expect to be given this seat, ergo voice, by virtue of our title alone. Often, we must demonstrate genuine interest, offer something useful back and then advocate for, before being offered a seat at the business table. All these steps are facilitated by always listening.

As HR business partners, the growth and learning we seek through this type of listening is that which makes us more useful to the business because we have listened to the extent of developing real understanding. We are already pre-qualified to speak regarding matters relating to the HR function, so here I am referring to being qualified to speak on the specific idiosyncrasies of the people within a business area and the associated matters arising therein. We can build many powerful interventions from the seat of real understanding.

At a basic level, real understanding, developed through deep listening, gives us an ability to foresee the implications of certain decisions. Always listening creates knowledge, and this knowledge allows an enhanced vision, which in turn provides a greater accuracy to inform decision making. The simple principle here *in extremis* being that if a person knew all there was to know then they would surely, usually, make very good decisions.

As a people group who trade our wares principally as 'expert advisors', this is a desirable position to attain – the people-expert advisor who provides accurate, coherent and well-informed counsel to business leaders at key decision-making junctures. This is indisputably an example of value-add. Always listening will enable us to achieve this lofty acclaim.

The creation of credibility

The third use of listening for us is closely related to the second. Always listening for the purposes of growth and learning means that our natural destination will be to become a business advocate with a seat, and a voice, at the table. These traits lead us to the creation of credibility. A necessary reminder here that we are considering principles over methods. Nailing down the second use of always listening, and thereby delivering astute and insightful input to key decisions, will certainly support the development of credibility beyond that which we hold simply by being a representative of the corporate HR function.

However, the creation of credibility through the discipline of always listening can be a very subtle journey, which takes time. We should see this process as a lifelong journey to be continually navigate. Everything we do should be taking us one step further down 'integrity road', ensuring that we cement our place as a trusted partner. We can never take our eye off our own credibility, much like a game of snakes and ladders (or mostly just snakes for the purpose of this analogy), and there are a multitude of complex scenarios that can lead to taking backwards steps, hence the phrase, 'losing all credibility'. Ensuring we are always listening is one of our insurance policies against the potential loss of credibility.

To help us to appreciate this point it is beneficial to reflect upon the inverse point: the person who fails in the discipline of always listening will ultimately travel on the road of lessening credibility. Applying this directly to our role we must consider the familiar individual who talks before they have listened.

I believe this flawed approach of talking before listening can be interpreted to mean one of only three things when it is used within an HR context:

1 What the speaker has to say is procedural, transactional and cannot be changed even if a profound thought were offered – therefore the idea of listening first before speaking is redundant.

2 The person is operating a 'cookie cutter' service or set of offerings. The product is a little more refined and nuanced than the procedures in the first example, but ultimately listening is only required to use the speaker's words against them to demonstrate that they need their special cookie to be cut in the way that all the other cookies always have been (and always will be) cut.

3 The blind assumption that listening is not required because you (the business) do not have what I have or know what I know – knowing better than the business may be fine, we just shouldn't admit it or draw their attention to it at the expense of listening first. In my opinion, this one is the most abhorrent of the three.

Unfortunately, I have seen all three of these approaches applied in everyday HR practice and, in my experience, it is likely that HR professionals are still applying all three approaches to a lesser or greater extent today. However, these three traits are by no means unique to HR professionals.

Considering the three approaches set out above, I do not believe they would take people far down the road of credibility. It is not enough for us just to give the right answer, as those examples present. In order to create true credibility, we need to instead provide the right solutions. These two outcomes are seldom the same and it is our enthusiasm as HR business partners that ensures we have listened well enough to be able to know the right answer but ultimately deliver the right solution.

As touched upon earlier, it is powerful interventions that we are required to initiate and sustain, in pursuit of beneficial change. It will be a problem for us if there are people-related issues blocking or preventing the delivery of such an intervention. It is not uncommon for many 'people mountains' to have to be levelled before a powerful intervention can be initiated or sustained within a business. These people mountains usually stand in opposition to the 'shiny new thing', which is an ever-present feature where change is concerned. This opposition can often sound logical, commonsensical and exceedingly effable. Therefore, the subtle creation of credibility, through the form of comprehensive listening, is essential in this battleground for influencing hearts and minds over to the new direction of travel. There are of course many other skills and techniques to be deployed in the pursuit of influencing a person or groups of people to a cause, here we are just dealing with how to use and apply listening to this end.

Think listen

Listening, for the HR business partner, is not just a skill to be developed it is first a mindset. I hope I have gone some way to illustrating this point here. We must first think that we should listen. It must be a default position for us to always be listening. Our role as business partners leads us to be like guests in another person's house: we find ourselves part of a business area leadership team despite having no specialist skill or knowledge of that business. Our specialism is people so we cannot assume to base our knowledge and credibility in other subjects. Our first and perpetual thought must be to listen. If we neglect the importance of always listening, we risk undermining not only our own position but that of the HR function we represent.

It is this ingrained mindset, applied always and in every circumstance with all people, when on-guard and caught off-guard, which will develop our own knowledge and understanding, which in turn will truly build concrete and sustainable credibility amongst our peers and business leaders alike. Always listening can be applied in every circumstance and works just as well in every season, its potency never fades or diminishes and its ability to build bridges to hearts and minds is unparalleled.

I think if anyone remains unconvinced about the virtues of always listening, we only need look at someone we know who always listens well to us. It is always useful to consider the benefits of something from the position of how it feels to be in receipt of it.

Summary

In summary, to be successful we must be constantly predisposed to listening in all that we do. To begin with we need to adopt a kind of humility that permits us to do a great deal more listening than speaking – embracing the power of silence enables learning. Practically, we can harness listening to allow us to think critically and construct answers to difficult problems in the moment. Being a generous listener is the tool that unlocks a deeper understanding of the business. Our willingness to always listen and grow in our knowledge of the business is integral to building trust and credibility. The knowledge that we develop through always listening can be used to inform decision making. In this way we should aim to be the people-expert advisor who provides accurate and well-informed counsel to business leaders at key decision-making junctures. Providing this effective counsel will lead to the creation of credibility, trust and confidence. Finally, this kind of thinking is a mindset not a task. We must always be thinking 'listen', to ensure that we are always listening.

Let's move onto explore our next people fundamental, the power of empathy.

05

The power of empathy

A quick reminder and recap of where we are with our principles and how they fit together to make the whole being. We are first building on the cornerstone of 'knowing HR', to which we have already added the knowledge of the business, and completed the foundational triangular shaped inter-dependent structure by 'adding value'.

In Part Two I am focusing on what I consider to be the people fundamentals for the HR business partner. Our first fundamental turned our attention to the business of people by considering how to 'always listen' to them, in all places and at all times. To help us to continue thinking about fundamentals in a practical sense, I will provide a working example that I hope all HR functions will be familiar with. The simple principle is this: HR can be trusted to be a fair and independent voice. Practically, this means if an employee wants to speak to someone in HR about an issue they are having, then that option is *always* available to them. This is the employee's prerogative. That request can never be denied. This is a practical example of a fundamental principle. Therefore, we should consider our people fundamentals to be similarly uncompromising in application.

Our first people fundamental included the instruction to *always* listen. Now, with the subject of empathy, we must dig deeper beyond the merits of always listening, to a place where we can intrinsically access, understand, feel and explain what sits behind the responses we see in our people. This is no small task and is unlikely to be perfected overnight. We must learn and understand empathy as a concept before we can begin to practise it to better interpret the people within our businesses.

The definition

Empathy can be a slippery subject. It is a word familiar to all of us and sometimes this familiarity can mean we think we understand it better than perhaps we really do. A kind of unintentional complacency can easily form. When trying to understand something more deeply, I always find it useful to strip things back to their original meaning, and not what we think they mean. In our roles our words are important, so it is essential we fully understand their meanings. For this it is useful to begin by taking a rudimentary tour through the dictionary to consider the respective definitions of two relevant and related terms: 1) the definition of empathy itself; and 2) the definition of sympathy. The respective definitions are as follows:

> Empathy is the ability to share another person's feelings and emotions as if they were your own. (Collins, 2021a)

> If you have sympathy for someone who is in a bad situation, you are sorry for them, and show this in the way you behave towards them. (Collins, 2021b)

The first thing that jumps off the page when we read these two definitions concurrently is that empathy is an ability and that sympathy manifests in a behaviour. In our profession we can all appreciate the dramatic difference between abilities and behaviours.

If we lean across to the dictionary's expressive cousin, the thesaurus, it tells us that some of the alternative words for ability are aptitude, skill, capability, capacity, talent, gift, knack, power, proficiency, competence and adeptness (Collins, 2021c).

It is an unintended coincidence on my part that I named this chapter 'The *power* of empathy', and that a synonym for ability is power. We will need to consider the power of empathy and an ability for empathy simultaneously and interchangeably in our pursuit of building trust and confidence.

Primarily, as we develop these people fundamentals, we need to get well acquainted with the correct definition of empathy. Once we understand the definition, we need to be in the pursuit of developing the ability of empathy. Hopefully, thinking about empathy as an ability, a skill, a capability, something that we can develop a talent, proficiency and competence in, will enable us to rethink our own adeptness for empathy.

I draw our attention to the definitions of empathy and sympathy simultaneously because they can often be blurred. Surprisingly, whilst almost everyone can explain the concept of sympathy, I find that fewer people are as comfortable, confident and competent explaining the subtle nuance of the meaning of empathy.

While the dictionary definition of empathy is a good place to start in understanding the important differentiating factors of empathy, turning our minds towards the development of empathy as an ability is still where we need to go.

The ability of empathy

Much like developing any ability, we must practise empathy to master it. Practice will make perfect, so practise we will.

It is true that some people may possess natural ability in this area of empathy. Perhaps someone may have a more natural predisposition, willingness or openness to process another's feelings and discern those emotions for oneself, than the next person. On this point, I have encountered a spectrum of empathy ability within our profession. This may cause us to speculate whether this natural ability is the thing being referred to when someone is described as a 'people person'.

Taking this 'people person' thought one step further, perhaps this quality is the natural expression that businesses are implicitly expecting their people function to personify. Throughout my career I have had countless number of conversations with slightly bemused managers who remark upon the apparent paradox of the HR function that seemingly lacks an abundance of 'people persons'. The irony of an HR professional who lacks soft skills is never lost on the wider business, which says something worth considering about their expectations of HR professionals. It certainly seems true that businesses have an unspoken and very natural expectation that, when dealing with their

HR function, they might be likely to find some rather engaging individuals who have a genuine interest in people. An individual who is naturally more predisposed (before any training or practising) to 'share another person's feelings and emotions as if they were [their] own' (Collins, 2021a), would surely be more likely than most to satisfy this implicit business expectation of the people function.

THE GIP DEPARTMENT

A genuine interest in people. HR functions should spend more time than they do on contemplating these four words together: genuine-interest-in-people.

I have seen little evidence of much emphasis placed on the idea of an HR professional having this prerequisite quality. To me it seems an essential element in fostering the ability of empathy. How can we solve this conundrum and break the paradox of a people department without a natural and genuine interest in people?

Perhaps in pursuit of a solution we should make this into a three-letter-acronym so that the business pays attention: GIP. Once acronymized perhaps we could introduce it as a new programme to be rolled out across the function? Maybe that will fix the problem.

I sometimes think we should rename the HR function, and many organizations have already taken this step. However, versions of the people department or the people and culture department are still not descriptive enough to remind people what we should be doing. Perhaps renaming it the GIP department will focus the minds and mend the hearts?

Perhaps empathy should be rolled-up into a standardized test that we have to pass before taking up a role in the people profession. I would certainly be in favour of this approach. Whatever the answer, I expect that a natural tendency towards empathy will stand an individual in good stead for the highs and lows of a career in people. Having an entrenched ability to understand the feelings of others is an essential tool in the business of people.

Whose shoes?

So, whether we consider ourselves to already possess some of this natural leaning toward empathy, or whether it is an ability to be developed from scratch, it is beneficial to consider how we go about developing an ability in something, which can be discerned, but is difficult to measure definitively.

I have found that the main and most effective way of beginning to develop this ability is to put into practice one simple phrase:

What does it feel like to be in their shoes?

The repeated application of this phrase and corresponding assessment of a person's circumstances based on how they describe them (and not how we think they should be feeling in these circumstances), should lead us down the path of understanding why they are feeling those feelings. It is the knowledge of the 'why' that will lead us to the honing of the ability of empathy. A little like discovering the value of 'x' in a mathematical equation, the discovery of 'why' in the empathy pursuit will help to unlock most people problems.

'Why' has always been an important thing to understand, whatever the circumstances. Mainly because if we understand the 'why' of something then we can authoritatively bend, change, improve or augment how that thing is performed or structured, achieving the desired outcome whilst still answering the original 'why' question in a more effective way. Many efficiencies can be achieved by understanding this 'why' paradigm. If we do not understand why something is performed in the way it is, we will almost certainly not be well enough informed to suggest a better, or improved, way of doing things. For example, consider progress at Apple, who released the first iPhone in 2007. Some might say that all they have done since then is incrementally improve the same product. It seems to be working out well for them though! Innovation may change the pitch, but progress is achieved through incremental change.

So, when it comes to people and their feelings, the appreciation of why they feel a certain way will open many doors and routes to possible solutions that may have previously seemed closed or blocked.

Any gap in the appreciation of 'why' will leave the hearer some way short of being able to suggest or apply effective or workable solutions to people problems. This is why, in my opinion, it is essential for us to master the ability of empathy. We are required every day to provide businesses with solutions to difficult people problems. We should be using empathy as the key to unlock these doors.

Therefore, we should make it our goal to become skilled in empathy through the practical application of putting ourselves in other people's shoes. If we find ourselves to be lacking or underdeveloped in this area, I suggest the remedy should be to practise the application of this simple phrase as often as possible, with whomever may appear before us each day. We will quickly discover that this practice can take place in any and every circumstance, it is not exclusive to certain types of person.

Tea and empathy?

I must briefly be clear here, before we get too carried away with the practising of our newly developing ability of empathy, the power of empathy does not mean that sympathy is a bad concept that can never be used. It is a common misconception within the HR function that HR professionals should be employing empathy *in place* of sympathy.

Empathy is the fundamental skill that we are required to hold and exercise, but as any seasoned people-experts will know, there are some moments where only sympathy will do. As the designated people representatives, we experience the highs and lows of the people who make up our businesses. We feel the highs of the podium and the lows of the trenches just as they do. In these circumstances it is not slick processes or systems that are required but, instead, just our own humanity.

So, sympathy is not to be completely overlooked or tossed onto the trash heap just yet, but it is to be reserved only for the few moments where our feelings must guide our behaviour. I cannot write a list of these moments for you, although unfortunately they often involve loss, pain and injustice, but if you have a sound judgement you will have no problem discerning them for yourself.

What's in it for us?

Where, or what, will all this practising empathy get us? Though there are countless benefits to successfully harnessing the power of empathy in our work roles and life generally, I want to focus on just two chief (topmost, primary, principal, foremost, leading) benefits.

Firstly, to set this in context with the chapters of this book, I will explain certain concepts sequentially, because they need to be applied, or learned, sequentially. So, in Chapter 6 we will explore 'The protection of perception', and in many ways what we have already discussed in this chapter and in Chapter 4 (listening and empathy) can be considered as essential precursors to the next principle of perception.

Perception, of course, is not the ultimate destination we seek, but merely another station on the journey to the critical destination of building trust and credibility. Building and maintaining trust and credibility is the first of the chief benefits of developing empathy.

I hope that by setting this benefit in the context of our quest for trust and credibility, it will ultimately help us to look up-and-out to know where we are going and see the bigger picture. I always find it useful to look to the horizon for future wisdom both metaphorically and physically. This horizon-gazing must be balanced with the day-to-day order of work, but nevertheless I am at my happiest walking slowly and looking as far ahead as the eye can see.

BEFRIENDING HINDSIGHT

Hopefully by now we have had some practice in applying the ideas in this book to our everyday people challenges, as well as retrospectively considering significant work-life events from our past.

If this is not a discipline that you are in the habit of, I would encourage you to start. Too often we are forced to test out our approach(es) in live situations with real people. As people professionals, we do not naturally have a lot of good opportunities for practising people conversations (especially difficult ones), to understand how people tend to respond in a certain set of circumstances.

> Instead we often find that we must befriend hindsight and do a lot of backward-wheeling-self-preservation in those difficult 'live' moments.
>
> Therefore, the practice of using thought to apply new ideas to old examples to see how they may have gone differently, is a useful one indeed. We should ask ourselves questions such as: 'What did I learn?' 'How would I do that differently now?' 'Where did that go wrong?' Hindsight is a good friend of ours.

I believe that it is this process of looking back to see how we can improve, with a sprinkling of new thought and additional wisdom, which creates the conscientiousness required to develop a serious and credible person.

Usually it is only when things go badly wrong that we have serious cause to turn our minds back to those events' ad infinitum to understand where we went wrong. In those moments I have often found that it was my haste which was my undoing. Had I instead really taken the time in preparation to share in another person's feelings and emotions as if they were my own, my actions, and the ultimate outcome, may have been very different. These are always painful lessons to learn.

As a result, I remain unconvinced that a people professional can be credible without an active and authoritative application of empathy.

As to building trust, as people-experts we must daily consider the composition of the 'trust equation' to ensure our actions align perfectly with generating trust. Empathy must be a kingmaker in the trust equation, because how can we begin to build trust with someone if we do not seek to understand how they feel about something?

Although as people professionals we frequently promote the importance of listening, we seldom talk about empathy, let alone create development interventions to improve competence in this important ability. I find this strange, because what most people really want is firstly to be heard (by being listened to), and secondly to be understood (empathetically). To understand a person, we must go beyond merely knowledge of that person. Sharing in their feelings and emotions is what makes it possible to begin to truly understand a person.

The mathematics of people

This brings us neatly to the second chief benefit of empathy – understanding people.

People are a mathematician's nightmare. There are just too many variables. The same approach, deployed in the same circumstance, with the same environmental factors, with the same person, can yield entirely different results in different attempts for inexplicable reasons. The general pattern of unpredictable human reactions can be unfathomable and baffling.

WHY DON'T PEOPLE JUST DO AS THEY ARE TOLD?

Many, many years ago, when the concept of the internet being used as an everyday tool was still fairly new, I was part of a team managing a disciplinary case involving an individual who had accessed pornography from a company computer.

The case became somewhat technical in nature when it came to understand what exactly had been accessed and how much time had been spent accessing it. So much so, that both the investigation and hearing stage required an IT expert to be in the room to explain the data as and when questions arose.

At one point in the investigation things got particularly tense and an adjournment had to be taken, the employee and their representative left the room and the management side, including the IT expert, stayed in the room. I think someone must have sensed the discomfort of the IT expert, given it was not a situation he would have been familiar with, and asked him if he was ok. What he said in response was both highly entertaining and simultaneously profound.

He said: 'This is why I work with computers and not people, computers are much easier to work with than people, they just do what you tell them.' What a response, what an advert for the requirement for a people-expert! A mathematician's nightmare indeed.

Humans can be a tough subject for the people-expert too. Therefore, an ability for empathy is invaluable, as it leads onto and directly correlates with being able to understand a person. Specifically, it is understanding a person and what they will think and how they will react in given situations, which is the key to our success. In the business of people, understanding humans and their likely feelings and reactions creates efficiency and streamlining of workload. It is those people that we do not, or cannot, understand who have the greater propensity to derail our work.

We should use empathy to understand people so that we can mitigate issues which may arise, but also to tailor solutions to best fit the people and individualities within our remit. This is a three-pronged prevent, pre-empt and predict equation, as shown in Figure 5.1. Empathy is used in understanding a set of people to: 1) prevent any unwanted or unnecessary circumstances arising; 2) pre-empt any erroneous management thinking before they become reality; and 3) predict an approach that is most likely to succeed. These are the factors that set our roles apart from others who may be responsible for applying a set of important rules, systems, processes or policies without reference to an individual's needs.

FIGURE 5.1 The empathy prevent, pre-empt and predict equation

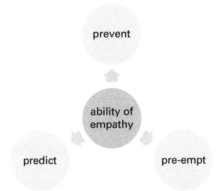

SOURCE Glenn Templeman (2020)

These three things, preventing disaster or unintended consequences, filtering out erroneous thoughts or ideas, and predicting the most successful course of action, are what will make us truly valuable to a business and its people. It is the power of empathy that puts these three things within the reach of the people-focused HR business partner.

This concept of the knows-everything-about-the-business-and-its-people HR business partner is what we have been seeking to cumulatively develop throughout these chapters.

When people struggle to articulate what we do, it is usually this often-unimaginable point, which is the hardest to explain to a person who has never been on the receiving end of such value.

Feelings over evidence

The effective application of empathy does both contain, and yield, a great and valuable power. It forms part of the 'secret sauce' that causes people to be perceived as affable and likeable. Affable and likeable are not popular or sought-after qualities in the modern world of work but, nevertheless, they are qualities that will mean other people enjoy being around us. I think that people enjoying our company ought to be an entry requirement to people leadership.

It is true that not all leaders are liked but if we have successfully harnessed empathy, built trust and credibility, and taken the time to truly understand people, we will be naturally liked and will have simultaneously built a solid and authentic platform from which to lead people. Unfortunately, too many leaders seek out positions, and not authentic platforms, from which to lead. Ironically, I expect that many of us have encountered instances where decisions are made entirely based upon how an important-power-wielding person *feels*, as opposed to any fanciful concept such as 'merit' or 'evidence'.

Over the years and throughout my career I have had several interviews for HR roles, but it was my very first HR job interview where I was tested on this idea of applied empathy. Strange or simple as it may sound, I was asked by the interview panel to explain the difference between empathy and sympathy. Twenty years on, I do not believe I have ever been asked that question again, in any context, which is strange because I know and observe that empathy has not lost any of its power in that time. Maybe after we have rebranded as the GIP department, we should mandate this question at interviews for all GIP department positions.

Perhaps in the pursuit of becoming serious and evidence based we have forgotten the impact of feelings upon our own direction and decision making.

Summary

In summary, empathy will be a familiar concept to us all, but it is still useful to ensure we understand its true meaning and how this differs from adjacent concepts such as sympathy. Empathy is an ability, because of this we can practise it to become better at it and develop it as a skill. To practise empathy, we are required to consider one simple question: what does it feel like to be in another's shoes? We must remember not to practise empathy to the exclusion of sympathy, as there will still be some moments where only sympathy will do. Developing our empathy ability will provide two main benefits: the building of trust and truly understanding others. People can be a mathematician's nightmare, sometimes our actions just don't add up. For this reason, using empathy to understand others provides us with a special kind of advantage to prevent, pre-empt and predict people's thoughts and actions. This leads to benefits including being able to avoid unwanted circumstances, mitigating errors in understanding and predicting an approach that is most likely to succeed. An HR business partner who can harness empathy to ultimately deliver these benefits is one who will add true value to any business. Finally, we cannot overlook the power of empathy as an attractive and essential leadership trait in our workplaces.

References

Collins (2021a) Definition of empathy, *COBUILD Advanced English Dictionary*, HarperCollins Publishers [online] https://www.collinsdictionary.com/dictionary/english/empathy (archived at https://perma.cc/N3XT-YJYK)

Collins (2021b) Definition of sympathy, *COBUILD Advanced English Dictionary*, HarperCollins Publishers [online] https://www.collinsdictionary.com/dictionary/english/sympathy (archived at https://perma.cc/L9BU-LEWX)

Collins (2021c) Synonyms of ability, HarperCollins Publishers [online] https://www.collinsdictionary.com/dictionary/english-thesaurus/ability (archived at https://perma.cc/V2RR-C44Y)

06

The protection of perception

The trust and credibility balance

Within Part Two, 'People fundamentals', we are pursuing the building of trust and credibility. So far on this journey we have considered the themes of 'listening' and 'empathy'. Now we must turn our minds to this strange little element in the trust and credibility balance, perception.

No single factor on its own is solely responsible for the development of trust and credibility; it can take an innumerable number of factors to build and maintain trust. To be on this progressive journey, continually building on relationships we have already established with others, requires a delicate balancing of many factors. We must think of these three things continuously – listening, empathy and perception – thereby balancing their use and application. These are the key baseline components in our trust and credibility balance as HR business partners.

As I've alluded to already, most of us tend towards a demonstrable desire to be perceived positively. We like to think that we are liked. For most people, this wanting-to-be-perceived-well trait of human nature is usually enough, in ordinary circumstances, to generate and develop the required amount of conscientiousness to fulfil the pressures of the social and moral code we find ourselves in. In extraordinary circumstances, people may not care what others think of them – if they are in a state where they psychologically consider themselves to be under threat, in that circumstance they may be more concerned with the primary human needs of safety and shelter instead of being perceived well by others. In ordinary circumstances though, we can expect that the fear of our peers perceiving us negatively is enough to motivate us to play our part and step up to the mark. At the most basic level, the presence of perception, and our own desire to protect how we are perceived, is what keeps us on course. Undoubtedly, these products of perception play a key role throughout our social structures, workplaces and organizational hierarchies.

They are always watching

Much like the adage of leaders 'always being watched' by subordinates, we are often made to suffer the same or similar fate. Despite the director or senior leader in the room being the one with the power, the HR business partner is also watched intently as if it is they who is truly driving the latest agenda (maybe it is, I will never say, and they will never know!). People always seem to be carefully listening to what we are saying, or doing, checking for any flaws or secret giveaways in what we might say, a chink in the armour that might indicate the possible future direction or intentionally hidden agenda.

WHAT IS THIS REALLY ABOUT?

Incidentally, this 'hidden agenda' accusation never ceases to make me laugh. Beneath the ever-serious surface I'm usually so stretched for time and therefore so underprepared for something, that I am desperately trying not to be undone by a killer question I cannot answer, or an issue of which I was unaware.

The idea that on top of my 'day job' I might also have had the time to work up a secret hidden agenda is ludicrous.

Nevertheless, suspicion will persist around the mysterious undertakings of the entirely average HR business partner.

The purpose of perception, which we must not lose sight of, is this: all the people we meet must trust what we tell them. Whether meeting for the first time or the thousandth time, we must be able to *appear* to know what we are talking about. Furthermore, we must sufficiently appear to know what we are talking about that we engender trust in others about what we are saying. This is not a subversive point. I am not saying that we need to be convincing liars. There might be occasions when we do need to withhold or soften the absolute truth, but those occasions are few and far between and should not be used to justify subversive narratives.

The point here instead is that the people of the business need to always be able to perceive that they can trust us. I cannot overstate this point enough and its application to all settings. We must always be on guard to protect the perception that what we, and thereby the HR function, does and says, can be trusted. An organization can be entirely healthy if it has an HR function it can trust.

Of course, authoritatively knowing what we are talking about and always getting everything right first time are the antidote to the need for perception in our principles, but as we have already explored, this is not always possible in the business of people. So, for now, we will need to settle for always appearing to know what we are talking about. This might sound defeatist, but I assure you it is an entirely pragmatic approach to a complex problem – 'appearing to know' is often the elegant solution.

A side point here to frame our thinking, we absolutely would not expect or allow this approach of 'appearing to know' from our finance team, but somehow it seems a perfectly acceptable position to me when it comes to people. I think because, as I explained in Chapter 5, people are not mathematics. There are no neat equations that we can apply to people which will always provide the same answer in each situation. In finance, the answer is usually x or y, whereas with people we could do x, or we could do y, they might both work or neither might work.

Obviously, from a practical perspective it is ok to say, 'I don't know the answer to that, I will find out and come back to you', that statement is still in line with our pursuit of credibility and trust building.

But remember that the credibility loop is not complete until the answer is sourced, and the person is in receipt of the knowledge. Not closing that loop adequately will undermine the building of credibility and trust.

Often, we find ourselves operating in the grey margins. The Finance team and the HR function at large, can both operate mostly with black and white. For them both, the answers to questions can usually be looked up or checked. Their equation for trust and credibility becomes much more binary. It relies more on adequately closing the question answer loop explained above, with a high degree of checkable accuracy. Whereas for the HR business partner, providing the 'right solution' over the 'right answer' can easily, and often, become a matter of opinion.

From perception to action

This is where the 'protection of perception' plays its part. We are required to always have what appears to be, at a minimum, a workable, sensible and pragmatic answer up our sleeves. At its best, this sleeve-pulled answer needs to be innovative, palatable to be saleable and galvanizing also. It is a big ask when operating in this 'grey' realm – existing in the corridors where opinion turns into fact.

Therefore, the way in which the sleeve-pulled-grey-opinion-sold-as-fact is perceived becomes vital to whether it will succeed or not. It is the grey that creates the requirement for the perception protection equation. If an idea, even a good one, cannot be judged quantitively then it must be assessed qualitatively. It is this grey realm to which subjective human judgement will be applied. In this scenario, objectivity can be a rare commodity.

However, it is not so much the perception of what is put forward that will be judged, the overriding factor is the perception of the person who puts it forward. The concept of 'appearing to know what we are talking about' assumes that what is being put forward is not a stupid idea, completely erroneous or factually incorrect or lacking.

If something of that kind is put forward then it doesn't matter how good a perception the speaker gives off, the perception of the idea will override the perception of the person (unless of course they are the highest-paid person in the room!). It is the perception of the person, and not the thing being put forward, with which we are concerned. The endorsement of many marginal ideas can hinge on the perception of the person in the moment we first speak them. We may only have a small window or limited opportunity to put forward our expertly formed opinion. Therefore, we should carefully dedicate our time to cultivating and preserving how we are perceived. Unfortunately, the business of people is not always a meritorious one, sometimes a great idea is not enough for us to succeed.

A general tactic that I find useful here, in the pursuit of achieving a high-percentage rate of idea-endorsement, is to aim to only speak when I have something useful to say. Most other attempts at speech are wasted and unnecessary and do not add anything much to the equation of perception, trust or credibility. Sometimes you have to say something unnecessary because someone has asked you an unnecessary question. That is not your fault and I will discuss this more in Chapter 10. The way to implement this tactic is to listen carefully to others and seek out the gaps that have either been missed or left out of the conversation. What are the things that others haven't thought of, and why have they been missed? This kind of critical analytical targeted listening and speaking will usually result in making useful contributions. If everyone always did this, I guess we would have shorter and fewer meetings. This approach of only speaking when we believe we have something useful to say will also help us to practise always listening.

I believe this mindset will allow us to restrict our contributions to those that are more likely to be primarily serious and discerning, thereby being significant and effective offerings. Hopefully, when put into practice it also results in one of those brilliant moments when the whole room turns towards you with that kind of half-stunned-half-bemused look on their faces which says, 'How did the HR person think of that (and why didn't I think of it first)?'

When thinking critically about speaking unnecessarily or speaking without really saying anything, there are some people who seem to actively enjoy this type of communication in the workplace, and it becomes something of a persona by which they are known. I would suggest that this is a trait for us to avoid. Instead, our contributions should principally be discerning, concise and useful to be practical. We can at times find ourselves in difficult or hostile environments where our choice of words will be even more important, especially as there is every possibility of having them quoted back to us at a later date.

If what we say is always being watched and listened to, then less is more in the protection of perception.

Perception in practice

Principally, this perception equation can be split into two practical applications: 1) perception when providing advice to an individual or small team; and 2) perception when providing leadership to a group. When I use the term 'advice' in this context I mean to include guidance, views, insight, information, answering questions, giving challenge, ideas, solutioning, planning, analysing etc. Generally, any conversations that we find ourselves having with individual leaders and leadership teams.

The two scenarios set out above are very different, both parts have very different requirements, and I have found that people in either part will react very differently to the same approach. Therefore, it is important that we recognize and understand the different scenarios and how others wish to perceive us in each. There are predetermined rules that we must play by in order to meet the expectations of each group and continue our trajectory of protecting the perception we have cultivated.

Perception in private

The first part of the application of the perception equation generally occurs in intimate groups, either one-to-one or in close-knit teams perhaps made up of managers or leaders. These settings allow scope for deviation from standard approaches dependent upon personalities, sub-cultures and historical norms operating within each small group or with specific individuals. Something about familiarity in these settings breeds more confidence in each other, or the group, to break from the norm.

Once we have established the way in which we interact with each other, either as individuals or in small groups, it seldom changes unless the personalities in the room change. However, this means that whilst these individuals and respective small teams can maintain their own norms and rules for interaction, we are forced to become chameleon-like, adapting to and fitting in with the different norms of each individual business area and team we serve.

These are private settings in which perception will be intimately tested. There is room for personality, and room to use that personality to colour the advice we give. This is a positive point. The more that business leaders can privately see the colourful side of a representative of their HR function, the more the image of the whole HR function will shift from the stereotypically bland pay and rations department to something much more meaningful and engaging. Make no mistake, for all the incredible things the professional-people-department is capable of, if we strip everything away, HR must still be the pay and rations department. It is not a popular idea, but I am certain that if we suddenly deleted the HR department the first thing people would complain about is not being paid. Hopefully, the second complaint would be the absence of their HR business partner.

Colourful advice aside, we still need to maintain a focus on consistently giving reliable and trustworthy counsel in this intimate group setting. If we are always being watched then observations will be even more forensic in an individual or private small group setting. A temporary lapse in concentration or of letting the guard down too far can damage the progressive building of trust and credibility.

The expression of personality is mention-worthy because whilst it is useful in the private setting, it is something I suggest should be somewhat tempered in the larger group setting.

Perception in public

I like to make jokes. I like to have fun. I like to make people laugh (just like Jimmy V said, 'laugh everyday'). I find it to be an enjoyable and memorable method of communication. Plus, I think there are times when the workplace would be pretty dry and drab without a healthy dose of humour to keep things moving. Once a relationship is built with an individual or small team, this humour can be applied liberally with positive outcomes, provided we are still simultaneously providing sage counsel.

However, I have found that this tool of laughter almost never translates successfully when leading or addressing a large group. I think this may not be specific to the role of the HR business partner, but it is accentuated by our position and the expectations of how others wish to perceive us. When addressing or leading a larger group, especially in any sort of formal setting, people do not seem to want to perceive their HR business partner to be funny. Often, we are relied upon to deliver serious news or pertinent updates that will have direct impacts upon the listeners in the room. Jokes in those moments, or at least *my* jokes, always seem to fall on deaf ears or create a lack of clarity over whether I was being serious or not (which itself is quite amusing if you think about it). In a relaxed or informal setting, such as a group away day, we have a much wider scope for cracking jokes and making people laugh (unless of course it is a serious subject!).

Instead of a colourful personality, and in my case, jokes, it seems these large groups may prefer to perceive us as 'the statesperson'. This 'statesperson' is always required to be highly professional and credible, not breaking from character or deviating from the corporate script. Trust and confidence follow them wherever they go. In this large group scenario, where an individual relationship with everyone is often not possible, it is instead the appearance of professionalism and being tested by the large group that demonstrates the credibility that engenders the trust and confidence we are seeking to build.

It may seem daunting to face down these large rooms filled with people staring at us, but when doing so we must remember the reason we are there – they need us. We may feel uncomfortable addressing everyone but that is not important as the situation is not about us, it is about them, it is for them. They need us to engage with them honestly and openly, to share insight and important information, for reassurance and guidance. They need to perceive us as the entirely serious statesperson whom they can feel comfortable in trusting.

A statesperson is generally used as a political term, and it is these hard-to-define political features, which make us put our faith in someone we do not know, that we are required to display in these challenging moments.

We may not naturally enjoy playing this statesperson role, but when there is uncertainty, change or a lack of clarity, it is this statesperson-like demeanour that people expect to perceive from their trusted people-expert.

Whether in private or in public, the practical application of the perception equation will result in engendering and protecting the perception of confidence. Throughout both practical applications the end goal is the same – for the enquirers and listeners to gain trust and confidence in their HR business partner.

Avoiding optics

Before we close off this theme it is worth dealing briefly with a widely overused term often associated with perception – 'optics'.

In the business of people this term is invariably accompanied by exaggerated tones and is spoken with too-high-a-frequency. This groan-inducing term is usually used to point to the potential negative perception of a thing, event, initiative, programme or direction of travel. The primary difference between these 'optics' and our theme is that we have been focusing on the perception of us as individuals as opposed to the perception of a thing. However, there is a connection between these two different types of perception which indicates that the use of the term 'optics' is in fact a signal of an earlier failure.

As mentioned above, the only scenarios where I have encountered the use of this term are when there is already, or imminently to be, a negative perception of a thing. My general disposition is always that of prevention and not cure. Therefore, it is my view that our involvement in discussing the optics of a thing is usually an indication of failure, because these issues should have been headed off at the pass. Or more commonly in our case, at point of inception.

Returning to Chapter 5, the three-pronged prevent, pre-empt and predict equation is designed to do exactly that, and proper application of this equation will usually negate the need for discussions on how to treat the negative perception of a thing.

As a reminder, the three-pronged equation is the use of empathy in understanding a set of people to: 1) prevent any unwanted or unnecessary circumstances arising; 2) pre-empt any erroneous thinking before they become reality; and 3) predict an approach that is most likely to succeed.

The occurrence of erroneous thinking, which paves the way to perception problems and therefore optics discussions, should be weeded out using this underlying principle of empathy. So, other people or unforeseen external factors can create circumstances that lead to necessary discussions on optics, but it is not something that we should be guilty of or have been involved in from inception.

All things to all people

So, the 'protection of perception' requires many things for us to match up to our many audiences, arenas and platforms of circumstance. We must be perceived as personable, engaging and even funny to individuals and intimate teams. Subtly adapting our tone, cadence and demeanour from person-to-person, from room-to-room and team-to-team. Moving from formal to informal settings, many things will change but the protection of our perception remains paramount, for us as individuals, the HR function and for the organization to be successful.

From individual confidant to credible statesperson, our perception paradigm has many sides to be mastered, controlled and protected. How you are perceived really is within your gift, you just have to know how, where and when everyone else expects to perceive you. Understanding and managing expectation is the vaccine to prevent disappointment.

Summary

In summary, the protection of perception is the next step on our journey to building and preserving trust and credibility in our roles. In order to protect how others perceive us we must first realize that, as representatives of HR, we are always being watched. This fact means that we must always *appear* to know what we are talking about. Often it will be useful for us to remember that less is more in these circumstances. In practice, we should consider how we are perceived in two types of situations, with individuals (private) and with groups of people (public). In private we are permitted to break with our entirely serious persona, adapting and flexing to the personalities in the room whilst adding our own personal colour to the conversation. However, in public, we are required to 'play a straight bat' and take on the role of the 'statesperson'. There is usually little opportunity for jovial behaviour in the public setting. In public settings the corporate script must be maintained. Nevertheless, whether in private or in public, the end goal is the same, for the listeners to develop trust and confidence in their HR business partner. If we get all this right and have already mastered listening and empathy, we should have little need for discussions on 'optics'.

Next, we are going to explore the concept of a moral and ethical compass, how this can be applied within an organization, and what this means for us as HR business partners.

07

The moral and ethical compass

I hope, if you are already advanced in your HR career, that I'm not introducing new ideas to you at this stage. If, on the other hand, you are starting out in an HR career, I hope these ideas are useful and enlightening. We are still considering our people fundamentals. These are the themes and concepts that make us human in the workplace and in this important business of people. To become a people-expert we need to continue to unpack the DNA of this people-expert-business-partner, to understand and harness it better, in the building of trust and credibility.

Turning to the subject of this chapter, it seems, and has always seemed fairly obvious to me, that the only function within an organization that can operate as the 'moral and ethical compass' is HR. This may be a controversial point for some, but I do not think my position on this is particularly unconventional or unusual. That said, I have had moments in my career where I have run into so much difficulty with this point that I nearly gave up on the concept altogether. However, those problems were unique to those circumstances and people at that time, and I have since rediscovered that everyone else requires their HR functions to steer their moral and ethical directions.

When considering other potential candidates to carry out the day-to-day operation of a moral and ethical compass, I find that internal audit is too far removed from day-to-day operations to be effective in this function. I suppose if you have an ethics department they may be across this subject in part, and anyone responsible for corporate social responsibility (CSR) will likely also only contribute to, and not set, the overarching tone and direction for the organization's moral and ethical compass. However, the level of involvement and contribution these functions play in interpreting and applying an organization's moral and ethical compass may all depend on your specific industry.

Rather than enter a deep theoretical debate on why we need a moral and ethical compass in the workplace and in business, instead I would like you to consider this question for yourself whilst I show you how such a tool can be used and applied by the HR business partner, as well as its benefits in the business of people.

Who is responsible

Probably, most boards and executive committees believe that it is they who discharge this function of upholding morals and ethics. They have a very important role to play in this, but I would suggest that their role is not of the perpetual-compass-checking-adjustment-advising type.

When thinking about who is, or should be, responsible for an organization's moral and ethical compass, we need to consider 'how' the strategic direction is applied to everyday events, and therefore, 'when' interventions are required in the arena of morals and ethics. Interventions usually have the greatest effect when they are made at the correct moment, hence the phrase 'just-in-time solutions'. We all know that unpicking something after the event can be very messy and painful. So, when considering the fundamental issue of morals and ethics, timing is essential. Exactly 'when' these interventions are made is critical to keeping on course. If 'when' is critical then we must think of 'who' is best placed to make these just-in-time interventions.

Boards and executive committees are charged with providing the overarching strategic direction. Generally, the primary role of the board members, as a collective, is to hold the organization to account on what it is doing, against what they asked its managers to do. The primary role of the executive committee is to effectively lead and manage the organization, in accordance with the parameters set by the board.

These references to boards and executive committees are made as broad brushstrokes for the purposes of our subject, and not intended to be a detailed analysis of the roles and functions of boards and managers. There are of course many more nuances on the roles and interactions of boards and managers, which I do not need, or intend, to go into here.

I do not believe the board and executive committee members have the bandwidth, individually, collectively or as two individual collectives, to operate as an everyday compass by which the organization can be perpetually checked and balanced. Most of all, they are not well positioned to make these everyday course corrections required to uphold our morals and ethics in the workplace. If only there was a people-expert embedded in each individual business area who could adequately understand and navigate these moral and ethical issues as and when they arise.

The purpose of the compass

It is useful for us to consider this compass concept in more detail. Firstly, when we speak of morals and ethics, we can often be drawn to thinking of a social conscience concept. However, there is an important delineation that I make here between conscience and compass. A compass is a tool that is constantly moving to point the user towards the correct route which leads to the correct destination. In every choppy sea, every wave and wind blast, throughout all the momentary and sustained hazards that threaten to throw us off course, it is the constant response of the compass that keeps us on track.

So, the compass is a tool and it is active, its destination never changing but the routing is constantly adapting. The senior leadership oversight provided, especially by board members, is more akin to the static conscience than the ever-pivoting compass. This conscience provides the moral sense of right and wrong upon which the compass rests and points its direction. One is static, the other never stops moving.

Explaining why a compass is needed would be the most self-evident and unambiguous task right throughout the history of maritime and sea-faring operations. It is used to find the way. Yet in business, this concept of responsibility for a moral and ethical finding of the way seems to be often overlooked or considered an entirely unappealing or dull vocation. We are not overwhelmed with people dedicating themselves to the pursuit of promulgating this principle. Perhaps we are just all too busy with other day-to-day activities to notice that we have lost our way. It can sometimes feel as though there is a trend away from a willingness to perform tasks that are important but seen as unattractive. I would argue that if these tasks are still important, they must also be completed with diligence, however attractive or not they may be.

Structural compass application

So, how then should this necessary moral and ethical compass be managed and applied? Just as the captain relies upon the ship's navigator to use the compass for course correction, so the board and executive committee should rely on the HR director. Quickly following behind are their merry band of people-experts, also known as the HR function, to calibrate and set this compass to its course. In my view it should be for the HR director, amongst their executive committee peers, to be accountable for leading this setting of the compass, resting upon the static conscience set by the board.

It should then naturally fall to policy-minded people within the HR function to quantify this moral and ethical compass setting into translatable policy. Which then leaves to the HR business partner the role of constant movement and adjustment of course, embodying the moral and ethical compass in all that we say and do in the operation of our role.

The only problem with this illustration of a well-oiled compass is that it seldom exists in the way described above. Given that the process of setting the compass can often be incidental or at times even accidental, clear direction from the top down can be lacking.

This risks the all-important process of setting and applying the compass being overlooked or missed altogether.

Of course, most people individually and of their own volition can be counted on to have a reasonable set of morals and ethics that are not outwith the organizational dogma. Nevertheless, when considering our people fundamentals, this moral and ethical compass is important and cannot be left to chance or the general goodwill of humankind. Morals and ethics tend to be concepts that are primarily thought and felt and therefore can often go unspoken. However, this subject is of such importance to the business of people that we cannot afford for its consideration to be only incidental, implied or unspoken. Intervention and action are required.

In employment law terms we might describe morals and ethics as implied contractual terms (although many contracts do have ethics clauses), but in real life we will need to be very explicit to ensure these are understood and followed diligently. There must be an organized and, most importantly, intentional, owning and operating of this moral and ethical compass.

Doing the right thing

It may not be possible, whilst occupied out in the business, to be in possession of a crystal-clear mandate on morals and ethics that will see us through every and any scenario. This makes it even more important for us to understand and apply the concept behind this moral and ethical compass under our own steam.

Being ready and able to construct and apply a principled moral and ethical compass is of utmost importance for us. This is because it is we who are likely to find ourselves routinely thrust into situations and circumstances involving people, where advice on 'doing the right thing' will be required. Our HR policy colleagues can advise us to a point, but it is us who will need to look the business, and the people, in the eye. In this way, we often become the arbiter on 'doing the right thing' in people practice, which directly impacts upon the application of consistency in people policy. Which in this business of people we refer to as 'fairness'.

This HR policy example of central creation and local application often causes the gap discussed earlier, between providing the correct answer and offering the right solution. Policies provide correct answers, but people-expert HR business partners must provide right solutions. When we become too deviant with our right solutions it impacts upon the consistent application of people policy. We must consider this fact and be mindful of it when undertaking the assessment of what is 'fair' and 'the right thing to do'. Therefore, policies are our friend in seeking to do the right thing, they give us the baseline that underpins the concept of fairness. It is a delicate balance to be struck continually with a careful eye on past and future precedents.

I am pretty sure I have never seen it written down anywhere that we are to be the measurer and enforcer of fairness in people practice. The problem is a positional one in that policy is made centrally, but decisions on the application of policy are made locally. This paradigm opens the gap between policy and practice. I can speak from the dubious experience of being one of those who has constantly calculated which policies and rules can be bent or ignored (broken) to my own, or the business's own, ends. Policies are often created in an idealistic bubble, and although we do our best to think through all the possible scenarios when writing policies, it is just not possible to account for all real-life scenarios in a succinct and usable policy document. Deviation can be a minefield, one to be navigated carefully, as any doubling back on policy decisions in the field will be sure to blow up in our face.

Even more reason to rely on the setting and reading of our moral and ethical compass to enable us to always do the right thing and be the reasonable arbiter of fairness.

Developing a compass

At its most basic, a moral and ethical compass can rely upon the age-old reasonableness test. This test is given to us by principles enshrined in employment law and expounded in subsequent caselaw, ie does the employer's response fall within the band of reasonable responses, and is this a reasonable response from a reasonable employer in these circumstances? This test is a good starting point for the development of your moral and ethical business compass.

Beyond that starting point, a large part of the development of a moral and ethical compass can be built from the principles we have already discussed. Specifically, 'knowing HR', 'knowing the business', 'always listen to people' and 'the power of empathy'. The application of these chapters should stand us in good stead for being able to pitch a well-balanced and proportionate principled moral and ethical compass.

If we have an authoritative understanding of HR knowledge and best practice, an intimate understanding of the business's needs, a penchant for listening to people, topped with the ability of empathy, then our judgement on where to pitch our moral and ethical compass should not be far wrong. Adding in the knowledge of the business will enable our explanation of the compass's application to be coherent to our listeners. Your personal knowledge will enable you to explain abstract concepts in ways the business will understand. I cannot explain how to do this for you, only you can do this, it is your business area.

If, after this process, it still proves a little tricky to develop a workable moral and ethical compass, I would suggest considering the issues that typically give the business the most trouble and assess the synergies in the problems that are presenting. If you can use this method to discover common underlying themes, for example a lack of trust, you will start to form the basis for action. That inquiry approach should hopefully tell you at least the subject(s) that your moral and ethical compass needs to address.

As set out earlier, probably the most common issue requiring the moral and ethical compass is the base issue of 'fairness' amongst an organization's people. Other common principles requiring moral and ethical steering tend to relate to commonly understood human traits and desires: honesty, integrity, transparency, openness, unbiased treatment, treating others as we wish to be treated ourselves, doing what we say we will and, helpfully for the seasoned caseworker amongst us, other general expectations that are borne out of the principles of natural justice. (If you are unfamiliar with the term 'principles of natural justice', it generally refers to 'the right to a fair hearing', and here I am referring specifically to the principles of fairness and reason-ableness contained within that meaning.) These concepts when applied in general terms are relevant to many, if not all, circumstances in the workplace.

A short side note on the phrase 'doing what we say we will'. I find this phrase to be usefully instructive even though it sometimes feels as though it should come from the lips of a politician as opposed to being commonly spoken in the workplace. I do rather like this phrase and find it to be particularly useful in the business of people. The phrase seems to have a special kind of ability to create a relationship between an emotion and an action. It works well as a call to action too. It seems a particularly hard phrase for people to disagree with, thereby having the effect of galvanizing people around an understood goal and simultaneously silencing naysayers. These are all very useful attributes to those of us seeking to engage and lead others.

Creation of a moral and ethical compass is an introspective task requiring serious thought and the application of clear judgement. This process, and the outcome, will be tempered by past experiences and coloured by current surroundings, hopefully for the better – these are the encounters, after all, that make us human.

Once created, it is not only the thing we will use to guide others, it will also be our own guide and measure through calm waters and rough seas alike. When the seas around us are wild and sure to swallow us whole, it can be lifesaving to have a predetermined guide and measure by which we can continue to discern the true direction through the storm.

Using the compass

It is a little difficult to explain exactly how each person should create their own appropriate and relevant moral and ethical compass; however, it is a little easier to explain how the compass should be applied.

We have already discussed how the compass must continually pivot and move depending on the situation and circumstances. Therefore, the moral ethical compass is best applied by a person. Someone who can use their humanity to make a human judgement. Our moral and ethical compass cannot be an object. It is a person, and that person is the HR business partner. We must be the personification of the organization's moral and ethical compass for our business areas and their people.

If we are the personification of something, then we will embody it fully. This is the best way to think about the moral and ethical compass. It cannot be put down and picked back up again as and when it suits – a compass does not take a break, it does not have a day off and neither can our own moral and ethical stance. If the moral and ethical compass was only applied some of the time, the principles would become compromised and the compass would be defunct. Consistency is part of its DNA.

The tricky thing about applying the compass is that no one is ever likely to directly ask us a moral or ethical question. We are even less likely to be asked to consult a compass. As we have already covered, we will frequently be asked to be the arbiter of fairness, but many moral or ethical issues will require us to discern them as such, and provide the corresponding compass readout in the moment, without being prompted or asked to by anyone else. Discernment is key here. Careful listening, always, is therefore necessary.

Knowing that we will not be asked a moral or ethical question outright, and the action of intentionally adopting the role of personification of the moral and ethical compass, should be enough for us to accurately spot and address these moral and ethical issues as and when they arise.

A small but significant point about the application of the moral and ethical compass is the way in which we tackle the issues as they arise. No one wants to be told that a course of action they are proposing is morally wrong or ethically questionable. This approach is not good for the building of trust. We must act definitively but delicately in these circumstances.

Seeing is believing

To explain what definitively but delicately means in a practical sense, I think the best illustration I can give is this: the moral and ethical compass should be literally upheld or held up.

When we hold something up in the air it is usually easier for others to see, it is also possible for everyone to step back and see the whole thing for what it is from a distance. So, rather than dealing directly with the invalid morals or ethics of a suggested course of action, it is far more elegant to instead hold up the known and accepted moral and ethical code for all to see and self-judge as to whether this course of action is in keeping. Let them conclude that it is the idea that is morally or ethically wrong, not the person. Of course, being able to do this with a group of business leaders requires some pre-existing level of prerequisite trust and credibility. Hopefully we are well on the way to achieving this level by this point in the book.

Needless to say, at this point, the application and upholding of the moral and ethical compass is a constant pivot-and-move exercise, in order to keep pointing people back to the ultimately desired direction. It is a marathon, not a sprint. It is not something that is measured once, but always. It is a constant back-of-the-mind check and balance performed continuously until there is no more work to be done, which may be never.

It goes without saying

I hope that this concept has adequately straddled the abstract and the practical to make it both deep in meaning whilst still applicable to the real world of HR business partnering and our business of people. I will let you be the judge on whether I have answered the question of why we need a moral and ethical compass in the workplace and in business. At least now we understand what it is, how it can be used and where it is essential.

This moral and ethical compass is a fundamental component of the HR function offering and HR business partner role. It is a classic example of, get it right and no one notices, but if it goes wrong, we will find ourselves compromised, no longer able to adjudicate on questions of fairness and, ultimately, with our all-important building of trust and credibility deconstructed. This very important principle of having and consistently applying our moral and ethical compass, is not something to be overlooked by any of us.

And the final secret of the moral and ethical compass? Get it right, and no one ever needs to hear the words, 'moral and ethical compass'!

Summary

The responsibility for operating an organization's moral and ethical compass should sit with its HR function. To create a moral and ethical compass we can first turn to what is reasonable or what constitutes fairness. From this point we can then consider other human needs such as honesty, integrity and transparency. These traits need to be well understood within a business to be applied consistently. The consistent application is underpinned by the HR business partner. We are the moral and ethical compass to the businesses we serve and to their people. In its application it is our role to hold up the compass so that others can see it and understand it. Not to make others wrong, but in holding it up we are allowing others to make judgements for themselves on the application of moral and ethical issues in line with the compass. Ensuring the moral and ethical compass is understood and consistently applied in all circumstances is a never-ending task that we will be required to perform week after week, year after year.

Next, we are going to consider topics that are seldom spoken of in HR business partnering – style, service and subservience.

08

Style, service and subservience

The familiar chameleon

At the risk of repeating what I said at the start of Chapter 7, I hope I am preaching to the choir on these staples of our people fundamentals. At least I hope that will be true of these ideas on 'style' and 'service'.

We have, since the beginnings of the HR business partner, been adapting our preferred working style, in a chameleon-like fashion, to fit with the preferred working styles of the different business areas and directors we serve. Being adaptable is woven into the fabric of HR business partnering; it is another element of the unspoken DNA of the role. Therefore, I will assume that this is a widely appreciated principle, but in case you have any doubts, I have set out the case for adapting our style to fit in with individual business areas below.

ADAPT OR DIE

A very brief summary for those who are less familiar with this concept: discrete business areas are led by a person, and that person has a group of people directly working for them as their leadership team.

Each of these people, the overall leader and the members of the leadership team, have individual personalities that require corresponding complementary individual and collective styles in response. Furthermore, each individual business unit will often have specific or unique, objectives, problems and risks.

The individual people, added to the specific circumstances, will create varying levels of differentiation that, in turn, will naturally require differing applications of approach to achieve universally required outcomes (like those set for us by the HR function).

Setting those points aside, usually director-level individuals have attained those roles because there is some form of personal drive, agenda or persona required or present. The individual factors exhibited by the director will dictate that others around them adapt to meet their personal ways of working.

If this sounds wrong to you, cast your mind back to the moment a new director was last appointed in your organization, assess what happened and what changed amongst the people in that department. I suspect there were a reasonable number of people changing their behaviour and approach to fit the new director's style.

Our role as HR business partners is to go into the business areas and work with *any* of the directors, leadership teams and managers we find there. Oftentimes with multiple different directors simultaneously.

This requirement, set against the points above, creates the obligation and compulsion for us to adapt our style to that of the business areas.

As we dive deeper into people fundamentals, I will focus on the elements of these principles that set the tone and position us for success and longevity. By 'longevity', I do not mean the ability to stick around in the same job for an incredibly long time, instead I mean the ability to feel, and be, fresh, current, relevant, open to embrace continual change and excited by new things. We have already considered the essential principles without which we cannot exist, now we will turn our attention to those that will preserve our existence.

Subservience probably conjures up negative connotations for most of us in business. Misuse of subservience can lead to many dangerous and comprising situations for those involved. However, we seldom pause to consider the upsides of this trait or when and how it could be used positively in the workplace. In this chapter I will focus on why it is important for us to understand and recognize the posture of subservience, and the reason continual adaptation of our own preferred style and approach is required.

Understanding the position of posture

Know that I always choose my words very carefully, which is of course a trait of an HR business partner. The word 'subservience' refers to a willingness to obey others unquestioningly. Clearly, anyone can recognize that a pure interpretation of this description is out of step with our role. This is where I prefer to think about 'recognizing the posture of subservience', which is not necessarily the same as the action of 'subservience'.

I find that, for humans, it is far easier to understand something once we have seen, or considered it, in action. Recognizing a willingness to obey, or at least the posture, the position, of someone being willing to obey unquestionably, offers insight for us into the intimate inner workings of a business area unit. Or perhaps even an entire organization. We can all recognize that, for us, subservience to a business area in our role is going too far. However, understanding the circumstances where others are acting subserviently within a business area will provide an abundance of knowledge on how our style and approach can be adapted, to provide the 'best-fit' tailored service to that business area. We need to be integrated in offering our services, which requires an awareness of subservience and how it creates belonging.

Much like with 'always listening', we should be applying this listening skill to develop understanding. Observing and understanding the posture of the people within a business area is essential in the process of understanding how our services should be tailored to complement the business style.

It is not coincidental that I refer regularly to 'serving the business'. We must keep the words 'serving' and 'service' front of mind when considering how we belong in multiple business areas simultaneously.

Who knows best?

In Chapter 7, we spent some time thinking about what we must bring to the table under our own steam, to influence and direct what the business does. We very much took a stance of 'in this subject of morals and ethics, it is I, who will guide you and it is you, the business, who needs to adapt your thinking to meet with mine'. We must demonstrate an awareness that this is not a stance which can be applied exclusively to all things. However, the HR function at large probably can apply this 'we know best' stance towards the business. This 'we know best' stance usually becomes possible, and plausible, when the HR function are charged with operating, policy, governance, systems and subject matter expert functions.

This 'style, service and subservience' idea is a back-down-to-earth reminder that we do not exist to tell business areas how to run their businesses.

The nuances between these two points are subtle and, as we have discussed already, this is where our role is different within the HR function. Our role is a hybrid function working on behalf of both the business and HR, to the benefit of both. In terms of the PR of HR, this is where we can do a lot for the positive perception of the HR function amongst the business. By virtue of our role, we take a different stance on service because we are charged with, conversely, tailoring solutions to individual business areas.

It is necessary at this stage to take some deep breaths and begin to keep any self-credited successes in check, so that we can continue to perform our roles diligently and effectively, without over-expending our delicately built capital.

There will be moments, sometimes occurring frequently, where we will require the business to change to meet our view, but the foundation of the relationship between the business and our role is based on the way the business works, not the way we work. This is why it is so important for us to understand the leaning of the people, the posture of subservience. With business areas, there will be times where we are permitted to steer, but make no mistake, we are always steering someone else's vehicle.

This brings us neatly to a key theme of 'style, service and subservience' – we must understand the unwritten terms of engagement when given permission to enter someone else's business area leadership team. If the business area is central and core to what the organization is doing, and I as a representative of HR am not core but am instead fulfilling a business support function, then I must operate as such when working with the business areas.

It is this kind of mindset paradigm that we need to understand and instil in ourselves, which will place us on a strong footing for success. I'm not saying that we must all be shy, retiring types who are reluctant to put forward our view or challenge senior leaders. Quite the opposite is required, but as ever, it is the way this is done that is key.

If we have the starting point of appreciating our role as a vital support function to the business, then we will be far more likely to appreciate the sentiment that it is we, and not the business, who must adapt our style to meet the needs of the business. We could explore this point for a long time and probably dedicate several chapters or books to unpacking it in more detail. However, here we can take a very narrow focus to this question. We are considering this question of who knows best in the context of a 'people fundamental' for the HR business partner. Clearly, there will be other nearby contexts where the HR function will know best and the business will need to adapt to meet HR.

Acting like a local

Principally, it is important for HR business partners to adapt our style to meet the business area's style and approach because we are joining their team, they are not joining ours. We are like guests in a foreign land, and as guests we follow the customs and traditions of the culture we enter.

Whilst the aim is to be perceived as a trusted member of the team, we must keep in mind, as discussed in Chapter 2, that we will ultimately always be the guest from HR (even if we seem to be a permanent fixture within the team and it is other guests who come and go). This attitude, of being a guest and honouring the local customs and traditions, will enable us to continue to build trust and confidence amongst the business areas we serve. This basic human instinct is one of survival – we naturally imitate and mimic behaviour we see around us so that we are accepted by others and not perceived as a threat. This is the posture of subservience in action.

Anyone who has ever joined a new workplace team will have experienced this phenomenon of behaviour-adaptation-for-survival. It is jarring indeed for one person to behave out of kilter with the rest of the team, let alone to persistently demonstrate different behaviours to the rest of an already well-established team. Anyone who has experienced this type of team dislocation will undoubtedly have the experience indelibly etched into their minds. It seems that as humans our preferred natural state is to be in relationships that create belonging, not conflict.

It is these well-established team relationships that we have the privilege and the challenge of joining. We will need to understand and actively apply the principles that we have already explored in 'The people fundamentals': listening, empathizing and protecting perception with a view to adjusting our style, to sufficiently mirror the leaders around us, without compromising our moral and ethical compass in the process.

Leaders of teams tend to value, and through the medium of recruitment actively seek out, others who complement and demonstrate a 'good fit' with the existing team's personality. At worst, this can lead to unconscious bias, which we must be aware of to avoid. The aim of seeking a 'good fit' only remains a righteous pursuit if it is not at the cost of diversity. It is this business desire for a 'good fit' that we aim to fulfil when undertaking our role and serving a business area.

A service business

So what of this rarely used phrase 'subservience' for the HR business partner? In setting out these chapters I lean towards focusing my efforts on subjects that I perceive to be underappreciated or misunderstood amongst the HR community. For this reason, there are many more well-understood subjects that I have neglected to cover within the pages of this book.

I believe we should always be thinking about our work as a service. When we have a service mindset, we start to ask ourselves questions like, 'Am I providing a *good* service?', 'Is my service presenting *value for money?*' and 'Are my turnaround times *meeting the service needs?*' These questions are valuable to those who are committed to continuous improvement and an enriching longevity in the workplace. Progression requires us to always be moving forward. Standing still whilst others are progressing is tantamount to moving backwards. Thinking of our services in the present imperative tense, providing, presenting, meeting, will help to keep us on track in the present and moving forward towards the future. As opposed to those who only think in terms of having already presented, provided and met the requirements asked of them.

The customer

This concept of being a service provider also creates another linked and useful concept for consideration – the customer. I find it frustrating that it is still worth reminding ourselves that HR has customers, and that we should be focusing on meeting the needs of these customers. Sometimes, within HR functions, too much energy is expended on meeting our own goals and agendas instead of making life better and easier for the businesses we serve.

There is an ever-nuanced relationship between service provider and customer as we move through the 21st century, and the idea that 'the customer is always right' now seems a very distant memory. We are now much more familiar with the concepts of providing the customer with what they need before they know they need it. That said, the customer and service provider model is still enough for us to drive action in the correct direction, that is, working for the customer to achieve their requirements. This is another valuable mindset-stance for the HR business partner.

In the simplest of terms, thinking of the local business areas we serve as our customers should change the way we interact with them and provide them with our services. We are already well-versed in the needs of our business customers and have already dealt with the concepts of how we tailor our services to the businesses we serve. Here, we must allow the customer–service-provider relationship to impact and affect the style and tone of our services.

Allowing this positional relationship to impact our actions is an overarching approach to how we conduct our general business, it is felt rather than seen. But it will manifest in small ways every day in everything we do and say.

The servant

To round off this thought of the application of service and recognizing the posture of subservience, we will finish briefly with the unfamiliar, and perhaps uncomfortable, term 'servant'. For our purposes this term means 'a person who performs duties for others'.

This meaning of the word 'servant' is in keeping with the spirit of our role and has parallels with the more familiar term 'civil servant', in that civil servants perform duties on behalf of the government on behalf of the people.

We, in turn, are thrust into a position between the HR function and the business, which assumes a never-ending loop of 'performing duties for others'. This 'what do you need me to do?' enquiring, diligent and valuable servant outlook, is another of the natural preferences of our role.

Ultimately, if HR business partners are here to serve the people, then we must serve them in the way the people want, and need, to be served. Understanding these concepts of service, customer and servant will help us to hone our ability to provide the right service to the right people.

One size fits all

On this subject of adapting our style and approach, to be clear, I am not suggesting that it is beholden upon us as chameleon-like individuals to become an entirely new creation each time we pass through a door or enter a different room. The point here is not the creation of a whole new style and approach for each different people group, but instead, an ability and awareness to make necessary adjustments and modifications to create the opportunity for a seamless and natural fit.

If we see ourselves, and the essence of our roles, as service providers, it will have the effect and impact of fulfilling our role and function in a way that is deeply valued by both the business and HR.

The HR function is a corporate function, and it must therefore act as the corporate parent. The HR business partner is the customer-centric-tailored-service-provider who translates and fulfils the agenda of the corporate HR parent, in a way that also meets the business area's individual needs and styles.

When we can adapt our style and approach, convert HR into a tailored service, and appreciate the posture of subservience, everyone wins, everyone can get what they want and what they need, in the way in which they need it. If we can adapt our style, adopt a service mindset, and exploit the upsides of subservience, our world will be a calm and satisfied place indeed.

Summary

HR business partners will be familiar with the practice and the requirement to adapt their style to fit in with the business leaders and areas they serve. This chameleon-like trait is part of the make-up of the business partner DNA. When considering the idea of subservience and what this means for us in our roles, we should think of it as a posture. Observing this posture in others will give us clues as to how we can structure our service offerings so that our style meshes seamlessly with individual business areas. In this battle of styles, we will have to consider who knows best on a case-by-case basis – us or the business – and traverse these relationships carefully, remembering our position as a business support service. In order to become a trusted member of the business team we will need to act like a local, largely adapting our style to meet with theirs. We will do well to maintain a service mindset and continually ask ourselves questions about the quality and value of the services we are providing. Performing our duties on behalf of the people means we need to continually adjust our style and approach to deliver deep value to our customers.

Next, we are going to consider our final people fundamental, which is the often overlooked quality of humility.

09

Humble headlines

The humble resources business partner

To round out Part Two, we will turn our focus to a personal quality that is often overlooked, especially in a world where self-promotion and stepping over others to get what we want is often the norm; as the title alludes to, it is the quality of humility.

I think it is important to point out here that this book is primarily focused on the 'how' of HR business partnering, it is not a list of personal attributes required to become successful. I will never speak to the specific elements of the personality of an HR business partner. In much the same way we addressed empathy as a skill and not a personal trait, here I will put forward the practical and positional application of a humble approach rather than purely humility as a personal trait.

Our professional community is vast and so is the community of businesses we serve. Therefore, when considering personality and personal attributes, the most significant factor for the community at large to possess is diversity. We have diversity within our organizations, across our industries and in every place where an HR business partner can be found.

Therefore, what the HR profession values is a depth and breadth of diversity to reflect the people the profession is serving. This requirement also filters to the individual businesses, each with their own organizational DNA, who require a unique HR business partner to match. This principle of diversity applies within our teams too – no one wants or needs a team of clones.

Within our community, humility should perhaps be the principle that runs a close second to diversity. Therefore, it is necessary to address this quality of humility, and the application of a humble approach, as it will be essential to the building of a successful, prosperous and resilient HR business partner.

Feet on the ground

As alluded to previously, our role instantly gives the holder access to many senior people and high places, and these high places can often be filled with egos and important-sounding people. It is in these high places that care must be taken not to become a product of our environment. A hefty application of humility, and a sound memory of whence we came, helps to ensure we can succeed in difficult situations and not succumb to them.

I believe that if we have truly mastered the understanding and application of the preceding eight chapters, over time we will find ourselves in a position of success and will become highly regarded by our colleagues. This is of course wonderful, and a brilliant feeling to know that you are valued in this way by people who know you deeply. You find yourself on the end of a meritoriously just equation where you get what you deserve. Many people are not that fortunate in their working lives.

As anyone who has been privileged enough to experience some of this success will know, it also comes with many warnings to be heeded. This type of success and acceptance often bring about a very large accompanying dose of 'soft' power. It is this success and soft power combination that can easily go to our heads and cause us to, unconsciously, depart from the thinking and approaches that brought us success in the first place.

When we consider the previous eight chapters, it is apparent that we cannot stop adding value, listening, empathizing, protecting perception, being service-focused and being the moral and ethical compass, and maintaining our knowledge of HR and the business, just because we have suddenly gained a little bit of power. The things that carried us this far will continue to carry us much further if we continue to tend to them. That is why I have referred to them as foundational and fundamental. If we stop doing them the whole house falls.

Soft power is itself an idea that we have not yet covered in detail in this book. It is a particularly important concept in HR business partnering, because the 'hard' power of the hierarchical kind, which can overrule others based on proximity to the chief executive officer or board, is not generally accessible to us. We hear often of empowerment, matrix structures and devolved decision making, but in practice, decision making and real power seems to come back to this eternal question of 'whomever is most senior, gets the final say'. Perhaps one day we will arrive at a new decision-making power-exerting utopia?

Even if this 'hard power' were accessible to us, using this type of power would undermine and contradict our mantra of becoming people-experts. Instead, we must rely on the process of building trust and confidence in the pursuance of gaining a standing from which soft power can be exercised.

Important but not self-important

This illustrious standing created by the blend of success and bestowing of soft power can lead to illusions of grandeur. As if it were we, and not the directors for whom we serve, who make and are accountable for key decisions about the direction of the business and its people. The feeling of importance, and the carrying out of important tasks, should not lead us to assume that we are, therefore, very important.

A quick reminder that I am writing from my own personal experience here. Therefore, I hope that you read this and find that I am not the only one to have ever walked this way, and if you find to the contrary you don't judge me too harshly! If you have not personally experienced this problem, I hope that you are, by now, wise enough to learn from other people's mistakes instead of having to exclusively learn from your own.

Importance is a delicate point because, of course, I believe HR business partners are very important, but what I am trying to guard against is assuming a view of self-importance. This self-indulgent, self-important viewpoint can skew many a person's previously good vision. There are many problems with self-importance. The predominant problem for us though, is that if we believe ourselves to be important then we must, by default, believe that there are some people who are less important than we are. Perpetuating a view of self-importance leads us down the slippery slope of creating and applying an importance-ranking system.

Yes, we are providing a service and so all customers should be viewed as important people, and yes, we do need some ranking of the importance of those people by who our primary and secondary customers are, with the caveat that all employees have the right to access HR at any time. However, what we must avoid is creating a top-to-tail importance-ranking system and placing ourselves in it. By considering primary and secondary customers I mean that we should not create a comprehensive importance-ranking system, but to be efficient we will need to be aware of hierarchy in the prioritization and order of our work.

This ranking process sounds harmless, and perhaps familiar, or at least subconscious. It is probably something we all do, as we look around a room, the office or the team meeting, and subliminally assess who is more junior than us and who is more senior. It may even be some form of necessary survival technique in some of the situations we find ourselves. The problem comes when this ranking process progresses from an innocent thought in our heads to practical application in a real workplace situation. This application can quickly become toxic.

We are constantly having to process information on people, or process people themselves directly, and come to conclusions to create practical solutions. This is a process that requires a reasonable amount of neutrality and a large amount of integrity to build deep levels of trust and confidence. If our thinking is tainted in any way by a self-conceited importance ranking, neutrality and integrity can become compromised. This in turn will impact our ongoing ability to build trust and confidence.

Judgement and decision-making capabilities become impaired this way when people are judged on their perceived importance instead of merit and sage assessment. However, awareness to the potential problem begets knowledge, which allows us to divert away from this type of flawed thinking and noxious unconscious bias.

It is beholden upon us to be trusted advisors. We must recognize anything that threatens to tamper with our ability to fulfil this role and avoid it at all costs. As they say, pride comes before a fall – if we are too conceited or self-important, something will happen to make us look foolish.

The application of humility to this situation, and others like it, will release us from the stranglehold of self-importance and the ranking of ourselves and others. This process of applying humility will instead lead us to simply seek to serve and support those who require our help, irrespective of rank or perceived importance. This is how it should be for those of us who are committed to serving others.

Making our own rules

I want to address another point here, which I have never heard anyone admit out loud or even refer to directly. Despite this lack of acknowledgment, it is not a secret and there are many people who are complicit in its existence. It sits below the surface, always present, a continual tension apparently never to be solved or reconciled. HR business partners, directors, leaders, managers and HR functions are all, at times, party to facilitating this unspoken problem. The point is this: once success is achieved, soft power gained, and trust and confidence established, the HR business partner *can* make their own rules. This issue is, as far as I can tell, entirely unspoken but universally common.

We need to pause here and clarify what we mean by rules. In this context rules means: 1) any actual rules, which means policies, processes, guidelines where it is intended that they are diligently followed, digital system rules and requirements (these are often the hardest to get around), and anything else that is written down, accessible and known by others; and 2) any tacit rules, which means anything that can be accompanied with the phrases 'this is how we always do it', or 'this is how it is done', or 'I know it's not written down anywhere but that's the established custom and practice'. The last point is worthy of note, as 'custom and practice' is a term that has meaning in employment caselaw. So rule-breaking, in this case, can be summarized to mean the breaking of actual rules, or subtler, tacit rules – the breaking with convention or established customs and practices.

Businesses and HR functions are places where rule-following and compliance are required. There are established ways of doing things, customs and practices, prescriptive policies and strict processes, all to be upheld and followed. The HR business partner has a key role to play in facilitating many of these and ensuring due process is followed. So how does making our own rules fit into that structure?

No one will ever tell us that we have now reached a position where we can make our own rules. Or that we can pick-and-choose which rules to follow, or that we can break rules also. However, leaders and managers will make this implicit request of us on a regular basis. Each time a given policy, process or practice appears to be at odds with what a business wants to do, it creates a kind of organizational socio-peer pressure upon us to 'do the right thing', whatever that may be on any given day of the week.

This make-your-own-rules approach (or picking-and-choosing rules, or, a rule-breaking penchant as I prefer to call it) is probably one of the defining features of the individual who is said to have 'gone native'. I suspect the two go together in the minds of the accusers using this term. It would usually be the HR function accusing the HR business partner of such a heinous crime, and it is the HR function who are usually most impacted by the rule-breaker. The breaking or bending of rules or the disregard for process impacts upon the HR function's ability to uphold the consistency of policy, process or approach. As we have already explored in Chapter 7, rule-breaking is a risky game where we are called upon to be the arbiter of fairness in the context of policy that is devised centrally and applied locally. To this point, I suggest that if you must break a rule, you at least break it consistently!

Regular rule-breaking can happen because there is a tension that exists within businesses, which comes to a head in the role of the HR business partner. In simple terms, HR functions want us to apply the same rules to everyone, whereas individual business areas always want us to apply different rules to them (only a slight exaggeration for effect).

The HR function needs us to fulfil its own mandate for consistency, and the individual business area needs us to facilitate the needs of its people. Both sets of needs are virtuous, but they often collide and create conflicting demands. This creates a gargantuan struggle over perceived 'right and wrong' and raises again the issue of fairness.

The chief rule-breaker

It is this tension that can cause the successful and soft-power-wielding of us to be prone to the pastime of rule bending and breaking. It is the combination of the HR function's reluctance to flex and the business area's various forms of emotional blackmail, which increase the pressure on us to bend, flex or need to break, the rules. Something, or someone, must give.

In Chapter 7 we explored the unspoken rules that we must uphold and protect. It would not be helpful or correct here to conversely explore the explicit rules that we can break, or even to assess the circumstances under which rules can or should be broken or bent. Once again, we are dealing in 'hows' and not 'whats'.

THE RULES I *WOULD* BREAK

Setting aside what I have just said, my duplicity says it could be a lot of fun to consider which rules we would break and under what circumstances!

The first rule on the list for breaking would be 'any rule made by the recruitment team'. I love my recruitment colleagues dearly, but they are usually the protectors and purveyors of many arbitrary rules!

The second one for breaking would be 'illogical rules that make no real-world sense'. Rules that seem to be 'made-up' for no specific or sensible reason. There are a surprising number of these in existence. In fact, now that I think about it, I have probably made it a rule for myself to only break rules that are 'illogical' or arbitrary by this definition.

In practice this seems to make rule-breaking much more palatable, logical and sensical for all involved, if they can see that the rule we are breaking is an arbitrary one anyway when applied to the real-world circumstances we face.

Instead, our focus is to be drawn back to humility. If we can absorb and apply a humble approach to our position, then that will act as a form of prevention against a susceptibility for breaking rules too frequently or too egregiously. Rather than attempting to treat the symptoms as and when they arise, this prior embodying of humility will treat the cause and prevent the symptoms arising.

This principle of prevention (or mitigation) is important, because what is required is an intervention to disrupt the cycle. The cycle of success, rule-breaking, getting away with it, and successful outcomes from rule-breaking will only lead to feeling a greater sense of success and self-importance. Humility can intervene in this cycle and prevent further unnecessary escalation.

Breaking of the type of 'rules' we are referring to will not always be inherently wrong. The point here is that within this paradigm, which places the HR business partner in the position of *needing* to bend and break rules, there must be a principle for maintaining integrity, order, trust and success. If rule-breaking is to some extent necessary, then there must be a factor by which it can be redeemable. Where it may be right for some rules to be bent or broken, it will also be right for others to be upheld. A check and balance are needed, and on this subject, only a human intervention, akin to the embodying of the moral and ethical compass, will be enough to save us from ourselves.

I believe that it is the principle of humility which will ground us in sound judgement when all around are too focused on their individual situations to make a sensible decision. This preventative use of humility is necessary, ironically, because breaking and making our own rules and getting away with it will lead to pride and the creation of arrogance, which are both opposite traits to humility.

Prevention is better than cure

'Humble headlines' is a reminder of how the upright HR business partner should be positioned and behave within an organization. This is how we ensure we continue the progressive journey of building trust and confidence. The message of this principle needs to be digested deeply and applied to our own circumstance and situation as a perpetual check and balance mechanism, continually providing a readout to keep us in-check and on course.

We are all human, and can therefore be allowed to make errors, but it is useful to remember that the role of HR business partner carries with it a high level of integrity, which is to be guarded closely. This integrity is the thing that is afforded initially by others and built over time to allow us a voice within the business. An HR business partner without integrity is like a castle without a moat and drawbridge – easily overcome. As the saying goes, if you don't stand for something, you'll fall for anything.

Humility, in this case, is to be used for prevention. It can also work as cure, but that is a far more painful route. In this case, prevention is protection from the pain of failure and correction. In the context of experiencing the pain of being humbled, it is the person who can learn from the mistakes of others, to avoid making those same mistakes themselves, who is wise indeed. Failure is still a great teacher though. I'll let you decide.

The application of humility keeps us grounded in high places and maintains our awareness of where we came from when we find ourselves far from home.

No headlines

The title of this chapter should be a memorable guide for us, because of course, 'humble headlines', means no headlines at all. As important and high-ranking as we may be or become, we must not let this fact affect how we conduct our services. When all is said and done, we ought to be able to quietly shrink back into the shadows of others in the knowledge that our humble support service has made a fundamental difference to the success of others. We should never be the headline act.

It is for others in the business to take the headlines, for us, it is being comfortable in humility that will set us free.

Summary

In summary, we are focused on the 'how' of HR business partnering, which, when it comes to humility, means embracing the practical and positional application of a humble approach. Success in our roles will give us access to high places and powerful people. Humility will be required to ensure we remember our humble beginnings and keep our feet on the ground. A mix of success and spending time in high places can lead to us gaining a good deal of soft power. This soft power needs to be used carefully to ensure that our new-found power doesn't go to our heads and cause us to make harmful decisions. Just because we may have become important and carry out important tasks doesn't mean that we should allow ourselves to be filled with self-importance. Instead when faced with this scenario, we should apply humility to continue to simply seek to serve and support those who require our help. In our roles, a constant and underlying risk will be the suggestion that we should bend or break rules in pursuit of 'doing the right thing'. Whilst some rule-breaking may at times be required, the preventative use of humility will improve our judgment so that we avoid becoming arrogant. Our integrity is to be guarded closely. Humility is the moat that will protect our fortress of uprightness.

That rounds out our people fundamentals. Looking ahead to Part Three, we will now be moving onto 'the road to strategic'. We will begin this new part of our journey by looking at the subject of procrastination.

The road to strategic

Our whole journey is taking us on the road to strategic, but here we need to take a moment for a very targeted house cleaning before we firmly turn onto the strategic road. Therefore, the synopsis of this section can be simply explained by twisting an age-old adage, a familiar business tool:

Stop, *don't* start, *don't* continue.

The twisting of this familiar phrase may sound grating at first hearing, but as with all things in this book I am not attempting to teach us *what* to think, but instead, I aim to teach us *how* we should think.

It is time now to make space by stopping, not starting and ceasing to continue with the wrong things. Thinking about what could be stopped, not started, and instead discontinued should engender feelings of positivity, elation and glee. Wishful thinking is encouraged here. This section will aim to lead us through an essential process to create a clearing in the wilderness. It will give us both room to manoeuvre and space to grow into our strategic abilities.

Having a mind consumed with the foundations of HR and the focus of our people fundamentals, when added to all our day-to-day tasks, does not leave a lot of space for important additional strategic level activity. Extra capacity must be created, and more must be added in pursuit of our ultimate people-expert goal.

The road to strategic will show us that there are ways to achieve this oh-so-needed time and space, without having to work evenings, weekends or whilst we should be sleeping!

This additional space is necessary to enable the right environment for the consideration and completion of strategic-focused thought and corresponding action. As the phrase goes, we must work smarter, not harder.

10

The active application of procrastination

The first rule of HR

This might seem like a strange subject for our tenth principle or for a principle at all, especially in the world of business, but I've been holding it back for as long as possible and in some ways it has been relegated from first place to tenth. It is remarkable that we have gotten this far without it being mentioned once! We are not dealing in rules, but if we were, I think we could consider whether procrastination could be the first rule of HR. Let me explain...

The placement of this subject at the start of a part titled 'The road to strategic' signals the beginning of a direction change for us. The first nine chapters have all been about building up the fundamentals of how to be an HR business partner. I still believe in the proper use of procrastination as a primary part of how we perform our roles, but as a 'how' principle it is also applicable to the entire HR function. Therefore, whilst I believe the active application of procrastination is an essential building block for all of us in HR, it is also key in creating the route to achieving the strategic position we as HR business partners are aiming for. In this chapter we have a principle that will equip us for today and clears a path for much more tomorrow. I will address procrastination as a principle in its own right, but mainly we should consider it as the enabler on our road to strategic. This principle is therefore a type of hybrid crossover of skills and preparatory action to get us to where we need to go.

Part of what I will explain in this chapter sets us up for that most wonderful thing – getting rid of work! Getting rid of the wrong type of work is something we must do in order to be successful in tackling the right type of business-altering-strategic-change-initiating-activity that we should be leading.

I routinely receive bemused looks and quite a bit of laughter from colleagues when I recite that, 'the first rule of HR is procrastination'. People think I'm joking. I think most people just do not expect their HR team to be witty and profound all at the same time. As I said in the Introduction, people just do not expect enough of their HR business partners! Although on further consideration, perhaps people are laughing because they think HR is systemically putting things off. I will let you decide!

I am expecting that you will be reading this with a good dose of applied scepticism to the value of procrastination, or even that procrastination could have any redeemable features at all. This can be an emotive subject, one that invokes feelings of pride in our own personal drive or ability to perform. When considering these types of issues, I can only share my own story and offer my experiences as examples of proof. Personal change will be down to you.

So, credit where it is due, this HR-generated idea is not my own. I was taught this 'rule' in my first ever HR role whilst I was still very young and knew relatively little about the role of HR. However, I think I knew at the time, and had just enough savvy to realize that this revelation was a keeper. Not least because practising it proved it worked. At the time the idea of the first 'rule' of HR being procrastination carried weight, because it was literally one of the first things I was taught about HR and because of who it came from.

Suffice to say, she was an influential character and when she spoke, you listened. It did not matter if you were the 17-year-old trainee or the sage already-seen-it-all-now-on-my-final-tour group director. It was her earnest and compelling style that made her assertions seem all the more visceral and urgent. Hopefully, you also have experienced the benefit of influential characters who have helped to guide your career to date.

THE PROTECTORS AND PURVEYORS OF THE ENGLISH LANGUAGE

Reflecting on this portion of my early HR career, we encountered another 'rule of HR' that has always stuck with me.

Whilst working in an employee relations team sometime between 2001 and 2005, we received a verbose complaint from an employee, which stated, amongst other things, that HR should be the 'protectors and purveyors of the English language'.

If my memory serves me well, this was in response to an error in a letter or something that had been issued by HR (possibly mixing up 'principle' and 'principal'). Again, this idea was not my own, but as a team we liked it enough that we kind of adopted it as part of our dogma. It became something of a shared mantra as we bonded together as a team over time. It seemed to make sense that the people department should also be the use of language department. Something about the very important connection between people and the words we use meant these two things, people and language, sat well together.

It has been tricky to expound and embed this 'protector and purveyor' principle throughout my career. Of course, as time has gone on, HR are not writing voluminous letters like we did at the turn of the century. However, I still find it relevant today that HR professionals *should* be the protectors and purveyors of the language we use as an organization.

If we hold the remit for organizational culture, inclusion, well-being and ultimately people practice, surely it is very natural for us to also assume the baton on how the organization uses its precious words.

A good, old-fashioned tool

It is worth a pause at this point to recognize that this principle was taught to me, and applied in my working-life, before the existence of the plethora of modern-day digital applications that have helped to influence and alter our everyday habits. All these now everyday tools promote instant response – Facebook, Instagram, Twitter, WhatsApp, Skype – but this principle in HR pre-dates all of them, it even pre-dates Gmail or Myspace! To think about the time when I was first taught this principle we must cast our mind back to the turn of the 21st century – paper diaries, meetings arranged over the phone and not opening the email client on your desk computer to check your emails until mid-morning were not uncommon features of the working day.

My point being that the world we live in now is instant, many social media apps allow for content to disappear after 24 hours or less, content is king, and it is often fleeting. Who could imagine not checking their email on a mobile device before they get into the office! There is not a lot of time for procrastination or delay. As a 21st century culture we have even acronymized feelings to describe the possibility of being left out of the instant here and now events of the day – FOMO, literally the fear of missing out! The only way to avoid the inevitable FOMO is to turn off from the world completely and to never know that all these wonderful experiences are taking place without us (in today's context this translates to deleting your Instagram account!).

LOOKING BACK ON IT

Whilst we are exploring the idea of procrastination, and reflecting on my very early career, I was reminded of a funny story of the kind that only occurs when we are very junior.

During this time in the early 2000s, there was an occasion where I badly burnt my hand whilst making the afternoon tea round. I had accidentally held my hand directly beneath the boiling water dispenser in the pursuit of expediting the tea-making process.

The net result was I had to be sent (you get sent places when you are very young) to one of the onsite occupational health nurses (who were a part of our wider employee relations team), to have cream and a comprehensive bandage applied. Unfortunately, the bandage (and the pain) was so overwhelming that I ended up having to take the afternoon off!

Not really an example of procrastination, more just plain stupidity! Really this story is a great advert for skipping college and university and just diving straight into the world of work. It is great fun and thoroughly hillarious, especially as a 16- or 17-year old! The only drawback is not having the lengthy summer holiday.

Hopefully this brief anecdote shines a light on the active application of procrastination. When we put off what we must do, and instead make time to think and reflect, we find that there is always something new to learn.

Despite that all-too-brief summary of our digital society, I find that this principle of delay or non-response is just as valid today as it was when I first received it more than 20 years ago. Whilst many things about the way in which I think and work over a 20-plus-year period have come and gone or faded away, this principle has endured the test of time and is one that I still roll out regularly to this day.

So, whilst I cannot honestly hold up procrastination as unequivocally being 'the first rule' of HR, I do think it should be a common tool of the HR function and particularly of the HR business partner, to be used liberally and in any circumstance, as required.

Before extolling the virtues, and general importance of procrastination, we must first bust the myth that procrastination is a bad thing in itself. Procrastination has gained a bad name for itself over the years. It is often used to describe putting off anything that would be 'good' for us to do. I struggle to think of any examples of the concept (or accusation) of procrastination being used in the positive. When was the last time anyone was congratulated or rewarded for a deft effort of procrastination? This usually appears in disguise, for example, 'it's a good job you forgot to do that then' or 'it's good that you waited to buy that as it's now in the sale'. Instances like this are often incorrectly attributed to 'good fortune' or being 'fortunate'. But the idea of employing procrastination in the active and not the passive (or because of an oversight) is a concept I have seldom encountered. We experience a version of active procrastination every time someone wants to 'sleep on it', usually a panel member after an interview before making an appointment. As if by going to sleep and waking again we will have a Damascene revelation that we should not offer the role to that candidate. It almost never happens that way, as decisions are seldom changed after sleep, but we love to sleep on it anyway.

To get the most from this principle we need to first perform the mental gymnastics to relocate the concept of procrastination from the 'bad-do-not-do' box, into the 'could-be-a-useful-tool' box, of our minds. I would hate for you to miss the benefits of this principle because you were not able to rewire your mind to see a bad old thing in a new way.

Whilst I am still feeling nostalgic, I would reflect on many things encountered down the years that at the time I dismissed as wrong or not useful which I much later discovered to be incorrect thinking on my part. The things that I previously dismissed, I found instead to hold merit. The key point is that it was me, and not the thing, which was incorrect. We should always keep in mind the role we ourselves play in the process of objective judgement. It seems there is a certain synergy between age and humility (and stupidity!).

The 'do-nothing' option

The first benefit to acknowledge within the realm of procrastination is that there is always available to us a 'do-nothing' option. This is neither a negative option nor an option that does not require a decision. Hopefully your recent mental rewiring is enough to prevent from losing you straight away with that thought! I know this is probably an unpopular idea. If you were reading this thinking that procrastination is anathema to you then the idea of 'doing nothing' is probably unthinkable! If so, let us keep our minds on the overall purpose for us in considering this subject – making the necessary space in our working lives to become effective strategic level people-experts.

I should offer a warning at this point that this idea of there being a 'do-nothing' option was nearly, for the purposes of this book, a principle in itself, so I'm going to take a small detour here to ensure we appreciate the sphere of choosing to 'do nothing'.

In a world where we are increasingly led by the drum beat of the 'programme' under the rise and fall of the conductor's baton (the programme manager), 'doing something' has become very important indeed. There is always a key performance indicator (KPI), a milestone or a deliverable on a spreadsheet somewhere that must be pointed to and risk rated to prove that we are all doing some meaningful work. This endless pursuit of action checking, and task delivery has perhaps had the effect of altering our behaviour en masse. Ultimately, businesses have become accustomed to taking the 'do-nothing' option off the table and I am not too sure why.

Honestly, I think we have created too many pointless jobs. Or at least, jobs that exist for the sake of fulfilling a gap which would be better filled by the building of a capability as opposed to the creation of another role. If it is part of a role's core responsibilities to create a list of things for the role to do, then that must be the definition of a surplus role! I am exaggerating for effect and jesting (a little).

We seem in business incapable of shrugging our shoulders and having the courage to: 1) acknowledge that there could be a 'do-nothing' option; and 2) coherently and considerately selecting and implementing the 'do-nothing' option. However, I assert again that we must consider that there is always a 'do-nothing' option. There is always a decision that can be taken to do nothing.

This is perhaps our second piece of mental rewiring that we must undertake in the space of a few short paragraphs. The idea of 'doing nothing' has to be put back into play, it has to be gotten out again and put back on the table. I think this resurrection (or should that be insurrection?) can be achieved by asking ourselves one simple question in the heat of battle:

What do we think might happen if we took the 'do-nothing' option?

Asking ourselves the question and considering all the various possibilities and permutations is not inherently risky or reckless, but all part of the due diligence required by people and businesses dealing with complex problems. Just because we consider it, does not mean we have to do it, but just the act of considering 'doing nothing' might cause us to alter slightly our overall approach away from the automatic course. I would advocate for anything that causes us to disengage the autopilot and carefully consider our course.

This is what I like to call the application of 'aim small, miss small theory'. Most people who have worked closely with me will know that I am prone to creating strategic and tactical business and people theories from examples in the world around us. This theory is one of those. The phrase itself means to pick a small target on a much larger target. If the option of responding to an important situation by 'doing nothing' seems too large a target, aim instead for the smaller target of *thinking* about responding to the situation by 'doing nothing'. Then one day you might hit the larger target by aiming for the smaller. In the meantime, there will be benefits to be gained from re-training your brain to think differently.

Remember, there's always a 'do-nothing' option, it just requires a little practice to master (as well as at times a healthy dash of bravery/obstinance/bloody-mindedness, depending on the circumstances!).

Reasons to do nothing

So, if we can use applied procrastination to master the use of the 'do-nothing' option, what will it yield us? Well, why do we need a reason to do nothing! Surely, the first unofficial reason has to be 'because I can!'. This reason does not make the final list of course, but it is always there hovering in the back of all our minds, right? If I can still succeed by not doing something, then why would I waste my time doing it! That is basic human nature right there. I do not want to ruin the wonderful surprises for you, but I will of course briefly outline the point of using the 'do-nothing' option here.

Firstly, and most simply, some things will just resolve themselves without our intervention. I will never cease to be amazed by just how often this technique works. Space and time are tools that we should deploy regularly when operating in the business of people. Sometimes we must also discharge the required amount of faith and trust in these people to allow them this space and time in the pursuit of self-resolution. It turns out that navel-gazing does have a business benefit after all!

That self-resolution could look like someone literally going away and solving something themselves, or they find another better-placed person to help them to solve it. Or, surprisingly common, they find that it was not a big enough problem to be bothering someone else with in the first place. That may sound rather flippant, but honestly for many of us our first reaction is to find someone else with whom to share our problems. We do this in the hope that another may have an instant solution for our issue so that we can go on uninterrupted with our day. This natural and honest human trait manifest in others does not automatically require a diligent response from us.

The second benefit of the 'do-nothing' option is the cover of long grass. Long grass, in this context, is a tool straight from the procrastination toolbelt. The ability to make something go away is not an ability to be overlooked. However, in practice it is far easier to use procrastination to 'kick something into the long grass' than it is to write something off all together (unless of course it is a problem that solves itself, as we have already explored). Use of procrastination to kick something into the long grass is often what is meant by the phrase 'keeping your powder dry'. In that, procrastinating on an issue prevents us from having to make a decision that could have undesirable implications or consequences further down the road.

THE DIFFERENCE BETWEEN LONG GRASS AND THE CAR PARK

When dealing in long grass it appears there is a competing alternative often referred to as 'the car park'. I cannot say that I know where this concept came from. Whereas, presumably, 'kicking something into the long grass' is a ball sports analogy.

I find that when we kick things into the long grass they tend to stay there. For the most part this is probably serving a purpose and achieving what we meant to when we aimed for long grass. However, it seems that putting something into the 'car park' means that we could also take it out of the 'car park' at a later date. In the application of procrastination, it is important to understand the difference.

We could of course always go and retrieve said ball from the long grass but the very idea of the grass being long is to ensure the ball is hidden from sight. The car park, however, appears far more likely to operate as a kind of filing system where things left can be easily found.

I suggest that if you do employ this car park tactic that it be one of those terribly confusing multi-storey car parks full of disorienting lights and conflicting arrows, pointing in all directions simultaneously, which take ages to find your way out of and requires you to pay a huge penalty to exit.

In many contexts it could also be said that using the coverage that long grass provides is a more prudent approach. It allows us to preserve the focus of the here-and-now whilst also reserving the option to go searching for that other shiny thing out there in the long grass later. We should look longingly upon this long grass as a tool to be used in the right moment for the right thing. Knowing and understanding the tools at our disposal will improve our judgement in the pursuit of finding right solutions.

This usage of long grass is more common than it may appear, if you have ever referred to or heard about the infamous 'too difficult box', then I suspect you have some experience of wistfully staring out at that long grass. The difference here is I am suggesting we should actively employ this long grass as a useful technique, as opposed to taking a passive approach, ignoring something and allowing the long grass to grow and consume it. As the phrase suggests, things should always be actively *knocked* into the long grass. This is a choice; it requires a degree of aim and skill to successfully 'get bat on ball' and find that long grass.

It is difficult to eloquently explain and distil these slightly abstract workplace behaviours into practical actions. However, the main underlying driver in which we all share an interest, is the ability to reduce and focus our workload in the pursuit of effectiveness and success. Have a think on that the next time you find yourself wondering where to start the day's activities.

Thirdly, and finally, you will find or will have discovered by this point in your career that not everything merits a response. This is especially true in the business of people. Sometimes the perpetuation of a dialogue will not yield a resolution. Knowing what to ignore and when to leave something alone requires sage judgement and confidence in one's own convictions. The more we can all work together to quash this idea that every issue (or email) always requires a response, the better and healthier we will all be.

Using time to measure our responses

Now that our detour into 'doing nothing' is complete, I hope you have reached this point and are hearing me out on the principle of procrastination, because it is the second key benefit in our role. The benefit can be summarized simply: procrastination is the antidote to reaction. Reaction is the path to pain. This is what was really being referred to when 'the first rule of HR is procrastination' was first uttered.

I like to say that a measured response is a kind of treatment to quell all reactions, it is the mitigation for antagonism. Procrastination has the potential to be such a powerful tool because it is the bridge over which we must travel to reach this much-vaunted measured response.

We do this and deploy the action of procrastination every time we receive an email, read it briefly (or sometimes won't even open it purely based on who it is from and the subject title) and say, 'I'm going to reply to that later/tomorrow'.

This is the simplest of points, and one that I'm sure many of you are familiar with already; it is a far simpler point than the advanced vagaries of 'doing nothing'. The simple point is this: do not react in the moment, but procrastinate, and respond later when the emotion has subsided, when we have all had an opportunity to think and a clear head with which to respond. So often, when replying too swiftly we are at risk of making a mistake or causing unnecessary harm.

This point of course is true for everyone; the medium of email shows us this. I know at least one person who has set up the sending of *all* their outgoing emails to be delayed for one minute after the 'send' button is clicked. The knowledge that accompanies hindsight has a habit of arriving instantly after the moment it was required. All hail the delayed send function! This active deployment of elapsed time achieved by procrastinating enables us to come to the right solution in our right minds and avoid responses that would cause unfavourable outcomes. We have all done it, and I am sure most of us have been on both ends of this spectrum. We have either responded too quickly and regretted it, or first gone for a walk around the office before we compose a response and been grateful for doing so. The latter is HR procrastination 101. I suggest that we should always go for these types of slow walks. If a day passes without a slow walk there should be cause for concern.

Personally, I aim to walk everywhere slowly. Anyone who has ever tried to hold a door open for me will attest to that. I find that a predisposition to slow walking provides two benefits: 1) additional time to reflect and think; and 2) it provides a greater opportunity to notice things that may (or may not) be going on around you, which may prove useful for future reference. These of course are the musings of an introvert. But as HR business partners, we should never be too busy to notice the people environments surrounding us, and to use this information to help us form evidence-based conclusions.

It is not that we should be immune to making mistakes, we all do and we all will. I had initially intended to list out my biggest mistakes for you here but there wasn't the time or space to do so (which I hope is an encouragement to you)! Instead it is that opening the door to making mistakes risks a far greater volume of work (or a greater length of time to fix a problem), and this chapter is about enabling us to prepare the ground to reduce our workloads so that we can focus on the key thing(s). If it is really key, there will only be one. However, I appreciate that in the current age we inevitably have more than one key thing to work on. But still, we cannot have *12* key goals. We must keep this point in mind when considering the use of procrastination – the aim is to actively manage and reduce our workload to enable room for strategic level activity.

So, the moral of the story is this, don't respond too soon, hold that thought, bite your tongue, it will pay dividends. Internal digestion is always more valuable than speaking before we have had a chance to think. That will hopefully give you something to chew on.

Retaining control

Hopefully this chapter has had some transformational effect on us or, at the very least, adjusted our thought a little in how we see and apply the action of procrastination. Or that we even now see procrastination as an action (remembering the principle of aim small, miss small)!

As to the application of procrastination, I find that procrastination is both a powerful tool to be used and a tool with which power can be taken. This makes it an important concept to be understood and applied by the HR business partner.

It might seem counterintuitive, as we tend to think of procrastination as putting something off, but it is instead a tool to be used to *take back* control. If the ball is firmly in our court, then the other player cannot play until we make our move. This is an underestimated power that we should claim more often than we do. Shooting the ball back as quickly as possible, or on someone else's timeline, is often not the best or most effective response in this business of people.

Summary

In summary, the active application of procrastination is an essential step on the journey to becoming a strategic-level HR business partner. Practically, the application of procrastination gives us a tool to filter our work. For those of us who have been actively using procrastination for some time, it is an old-fashioned tool but not one to be overlooked in today's world. It continues to work just as well as it always has. To successfully apply this principle we need to do the mental gymnastics to relocate procrastination from the 'bad, do not do' box to the 'useful when applied correctly' box. It can have an image problem that we will need to overcome. Even more troublesome for some may be the 'do-nothing' option. There is always a 'do-nothing' option. We must have the courage to acknowledge that there could be a 'do-nothing' option and to decide when to implement it. The first reason to 'do nothing' is that some things will just resolve themselves without our intervention. The second reason is the cover of long grass, which has many benefits. Thirdly, not everything that comes our way merits a response. Procrastination is the antidote to reaction; this is its key benefit for us in our roles. We need to be in the business of metering out measured responses and usually avoiding the temptation to react too quickly. Reactions can be dangerous under circumstances when only a measured response will do. The correct use of procrastination can buy us time, but it can also enable us to take back control, in our relationships and in our work.

Next, we will continue this theme of thinning our workload in the pursuit of making room for complex strategic activity by tackling the issue of saying no to work.

11

Say no to strangers

British readers with long memories will probably recognize that this chapter title is also the title of a 1981 short public information film (BFI, 2021) to warn children of contact with strangers (as well as many other similar short films dating back to the 1950s). This chapter is of course nothing to do with that but nevertheless the phrase symbolizes the mindset we are seeking to master. We are travelling on the road to strategic, so we are anticipating that the nature of our work is likely to be morphing from advisory and tactical, to strategic. By nature, strategic activity is longer-term activity. It does not generally require or entertain frequent tactical interruptions. This chapter is in part about avoiding certain types of unwanted interruptions or additions in the pursuit of success, strangers being one, but mostly about the presence of mind to say 'no', when only 'no' will do. Just say 'no'!

Conscientiousness in action

When discussing some of the ideas and concepts included in this book with colleagues, it is fair to say that 'Say no to strangers' was by far the most eagerly anticipated chapter in this book. Clearly, this is for one obvious reason: many people feel that they have too much work to do and wish to be able to stop or stem the tide of oncoming work. It seems most people feel they have too high a volume of work and they want to get rid of some or wish that they had never taken it on in the first place.

You will probably have observed that people generally fall into two separate categories on this volume of work issue: 1) (most people) will say that they have too much work to do and are stretched or overworked – 'there's not enough hours in the day' they say (to which I always reply sarcastically pointing out that they are missing out on at least 7 hours of potential work time at night when they are asleep); or 2) (a temporary minority) will say that they are extremely bored and frustrated because they do not have enough to do. It seems that there is no happy medium, and no one who enjoys boredom.

Or, to potentially dig deeper into the nuances of this issue, many people feel that their workload and priorities are split or stretched too far, which prevents them from doing as good a job as they would like. We should see this latter feeling as a form of conscientiousness in action. That conscientiousness is the primary driver manifesting in people's outward display of eager anticipation for some writing about how to say 'no' to others. Which, of course, really translates to how to say 'no' to work.

This may sound like a dishonourable or ignoble idea, but we must set this in the context of our road to strategic. Our purpose at this stage is to make space for strategic-level activity. In Chapter 10 we have just explored how to achieve this through the active application of procrastination. This provided us with a tool to put things off. Now we will need to have a conscientious heart to be able to say 'no' to the wrong type of work and flatly reject some of the requests that come our way.

I think also, and I will be careful what I say here, the secondary reason that people are so keen to hear what I have to say on this subject, is because they have observed first-hand that I'm fairly adept at getting rid of work. One colleague confessed that they were somewhat jealous of my ability to 'avoid drive-by taskings'! In simple terms for our purposes here, I have perhaps had a degree of success in saying 'no' to certain types of work.

Preparing to be strategic

As we have learnt already from Chapter 10, 'The active application of procrastination', this section is somewhat of an intermediate moment. This is to ensure that, having built on the correct base in Part One, 'The foundational structure', and developed ability in Part Two, 'The people fundamentals', we are now clearing a way for strategic development and the success that lies waiting for us in Part Four, 'The clever stuff'. It is entirely natural at this transitional moment that we be equipped with principles that will ultimately trim and tone our workload and offerings, to be set up to succeed in a strategic role or with longer-term strategic activities.

Trimming our workload and offerings is particularly relevant to an individual who has developed within an organization, come up through the ranks, or been promoted *in situ* (especially if promoted to a so-called 'strategic' or 'senior' job title). As touched upon in the introduction to this book, individuals promoted *in situ* are expected to flick a switch overnight and just become strategic as if it is all a very binary and simple thing to do. As if there is some kind of underlying assumption that 'being strategic' is a competency that can simply be quantified and certified, flicked on and off. Those of us in this position must find a way to shed our former skin in preparation for putting on a new strategic skin, except, in this example, the skin is a way of being and thinking.

Frequently, I find that the question of 'how to be strategic' is one that many HR business partners struggle with. In these cases we find that whilst they are struggling to grasp what strategic things it is that they should be doing, they meanwhile consume all their time doing that which they do know well, albeit not strategic, but nevertheless they can at least point to a definite uninterrupted ongoing output of work. It is the familiar tasks that we hold onto for too long that prevent us from progressing into this strategic realm. When we do this, it is as if we believe that demonstrating we are doing something is more important than doing what we are supposed to be doing.

I am not sure I will ever come to understand this strange phenomenon. HR business partners stepping into the strategic realm, rather than asking for help or admitting that they do not know what to do or how to do it, will just go straight back to what they know and have been doing for years. The only tangible difference is a new more important-sounding job title and probably more pay. Remarkably, this is not a new or uncommon occurrence. There is certainly no thought of saying 'no' to the old work in favour of a bright new strategic future.

I believe, and have found to be true, that the first and necessary step towards unpacking this troubling question of 'how to be strategic' is to create the required headroom for some deep reflection and strategic-level thought. Too often, creating time and space just to think is too readily dismissed in favour of instead ploughing on as before, with no extra gained insight or wisdom. We favour doing things over thinking about what we are doing. It is as if any task that cannot be time-sheeted is not worth doing. Unfortunately, as the saying goes, what gets measured gets done!

Starting to think strategically

That said, if any of us are having trouble with this concept of 'how to be strategic', then I suggest a first practical step is to free up some time to consider the following question:

> What could I be doing and what interventions could I think of, which can solve problems that the policy level of my current activity fails to solve?

Ergo, if it is truly a strategic intervention, it will occur at a higher level, or above, or over the top of, the application of all policies and policy-related interventions. Policies, of course, flow directly from strategy. There can be no policy, without strategy first.

To explain this briefly, the policy-level is providing answers to questions; the strategy-level is providing solutions to problems people don't even know to ask questions about. There is a marked difference between the two levels. One requires knowledge and understanding of the rules and how to apply them (policy), the other requires authoritative and comprehensive knowledge in order to safely chart a course for which there are few pre-set rules (strategy).

There can be no doubt that, in general terms, a singular piece of strategic activity takes up far more time and effort than a single piece of non-strategic HR activity. To illustrate this point in generic and simple terms, think about how much time and effort is required, generally, to resolve an issue at the policy level, even a complex issue – for example, in recruitment or employee relations. Then turn your mind to resolving wide-ranging systemic issues with the creation and application of strategy. It is those strategic-level issues that take weeks and often months or years to resolve fully, whereas many complex policy-level issues can be resolved in days.

It is for these reasons that we need to be serious about freeing up the time to be able to give a deep focus to addressing strategic issues. Saying no to strangers, as I will explain, is an essential step on the road to strategic.

When to say no

> I should be back in an hour, if my desk phone rings just ignore it, I don't answer it anyway. (Gina Linetti, The bank job, *Brooklyn Nine-Nine*)

Anyone who has watched the TV show *Brooklyn Nine-Nine* will know that the quote from this American sit-com, is a light-hearted jibe. However, if you find yourself stuck for ideas in the 'getting rid of or limiting work' column, stopping answering your phone is a good place to start. I probably stopped answering my phone around 2015, and now I do not answer a phone unless it is a call I am specifically waiting for.

'NO ONE'S DIED' THEORY

In the past I worked for an organization that had a system requiring everyone to hot desk and therefore having to login to a desk phone at the specific hot desk you picked that day. This really was wonderful. I discovered quickly that if you didn't login to the desk phone then no one could call you! What a brilliant system! I don't think I spoke to anyone on the phone for the whole 15 months.

This is a good moment to introduce another one of my conjured up and frequently used workplace theories based on the world we see around us. As you have by now already deduced from the title, this one is called the 'no one's died' theory. It is very simple, you try something that you are told not to do, or you break a rule, or decline to follow a practice that seems stupid or arbitrary (often a general custom or practice as opposed to a real rule). You do this because there is something to be gained by the breaking of the rule, often it will be in the pursuit of the right solution as discussed already.

You do not tell anyone beforehand or seek any advice on whether you should stop or not do the thing you are supposed to do, you just don't do it.

If you struggle with this mutinous idea then instead tell yourself that you will do it tomorrow, except tomorrow never comes. Keep putting it off and see what happens in the meantime. Try it for a day, a week, a month, and *as long as no one dies*, keep doing it. The exaggeration of death is of course for effect. But provided there are no definite downsides or problematic issues, just keep doing it (or not doing it as the case may be).

Give it a go tomorrow. It is amazing what serious consequences do not occur when you stop doing the things that are slowing you down. 'No one's died' theory is a useful side hustle in the business of saying 'no' to people.

Some people will, I'm sure, be operating in environments and cultures where the phone is essential. As a further reminder though, at this point in our journey we are moving along 'the road to strategic'. This means that what we do here is preparatory to arriving at the destination of strategic HR business partnering services. As I said, I have not answered the phone to an unexpected caller for at least six years now. I do not believe that this kind of compulsion for answering the phone to whomever may be calling, can be routinely described as a strategic-level service.

Anyway, this chapter is not about answering the phone, it is about the art of saying 'no'. We can, and should, become rather excited at the prospect of potentially reducing our current workload or shedding those frustrating tasks that add no value for us to do them. However, the key point, that people in their glee often forget about at the attractive proposition of saying 'no', and waving goodbye to some painful or pointless piece of work, is this:

> If you are going to say 'no' to work then you had better be sure to be
> very good at the things you say 'yes' to.

So, to ensure that we are taking a balanced view, we should keep in mind that this principle, whilst highly attractive and very necessary, is almost certain to heap extra pressure on us to succeed in all that we are doing or elect to do. You can have the freedom and capacity you need to do a great job, but it comes at a price.

That price can be equated to what I have referred to previously as 'being competent'. To be considered competent, we will need to have mastered HR, know the business, be seen to add value and have used all of the people fundamentals to build and engender trust and confidence. Trust and confidence that have been developed in this way ought to be strong and credible. This strength and credibility of trust means that even if we occasionally say 'no' to what the business asks of us, the outcome will be positive, as the business response will likely be a version of, 'I don't like this answer but I trust you and I know you are very credible, so, on that basis, I'm willing to go with what you are saying on this.'

Conversely, if we say 'no' to certain work but then also perform our remaining activity badly, we can expect to have trouble ahead. Turning away work and then performing badly at what you have left is the basis of incompetence. Applying the tools that we have discussed thus far will enable us to avoid this test of incompetence being used on us!

Suffice to say, we should have a degree of objective certainty in our competence and high-performing ability before entering the realm of self-selecting our workload. At times we will need this trust, confidence and credibility from the HR function, and the business, to permit us to say 'no' with the same frequency and veracity that we have previously said 'yes'.

Again, this will be an issue for those of us who are promoted *in situ*. If you have spent your whole tenure at an organization in a more junior position saying 'yes' to those around you, to suddenly wake up one day and start saying 'no' will be very difficult. Not so much because of having to change your own behaviour, but more because it requires the others around you to change theirs too. Changing your behaviour is within your control, changing others' behaviour is out of your control and is for others, not you, to do. Unfortunately, though, you will have to instigate the process for them to change their behaviour.

To say 'no' to work is to say to the requester that you know better than they what is best for you, and therefore the organization, to spend time on. This question of saying 'no' often comes down to time and resources. When moving toward the strategic realm there are many 'good' things that we could be spending our time on. Having a focused mind, clarity of thought and clear organizational objectives are essential in the prioritization of our time. This idea that we might know better than the requester how our time should be spent is a delicate balance, one that should be recalled to mind every time 'no' is on the lips. To this end, we must always be thinking about the implications of our actions, particularly the impact on our business relationships, the building of trust and the maintaining of credibility and perception.

Therefore, 'no' is to be deployed carefully and with great diligence with definite reference to that truly greater activity which must be preserved ahead of this new or off-piste distraction that is to be refused.

Staying focused and standing firm

The heart behind this principle is to bring us to a place where we have the courage of our convictions in what we *are already* doing, to know when to avoid those things that will detract from our predetermined path to successful delivery.

This is a point that we should not gloss over too quickly. When we say 'no' it must obviously be accompanied by an explanation. That explanation, I believe, will always take the approximate form of, 'no, because what I am doing now is more important'. When we make a statement like that, we should have a prior degree of certainty that the person we are saying it to will agree with us. This requires our three-pronged empathy prevent, pre-empt, and predict equation set out in Chapter 5. To be clear, in practice I mean that simply informing someone of what we *are already working on* should be enough for them to realize that their thing is a lower priority and therefore merits the rebuff.

The practical application of this 'no' will need to be followed by a contextually important word: 'because'. Failing to provide other humans with a rationale for saying 'no' is out of sync with our role as the people-expert. Nothing we believe in should be too difficult to justify to another person. We must have confidence in our own abilities, particularly in the power of empathy, to understand others and present arguments that will chime with their individual ways of thinking.

In these often tricky 'saying no' scenarios, 'because' is the bridge between the opposing viewpoints of two different people. The 'no' comes first but the prominence must be given to the rationale and reasons. The person must leave hearing 'why' and not thinking 'they told me "no"'.

Obviously, we do not want to act in a dictatorial way. This is where our people fundamentals come into their own. The application of these fundamentals ensures that even when rejecting the requests of others, we are able to do it in a way that continues to build our own trust and credibility within the business.

Becoming articulate in the description of organizational priority is a required skill for us to attain. The ability to accurately connect the dots for others between what we are doing, and how it gets us all to our shared goal, is essential in pursuit of turning away that which will detract from successfully achieving organizational change.

Development of this skill is also essential to enable us to educate others and helping them connect the dots between the individual business area activity and the organization's overarching goals.

We cannot, and should not, offer a 'no' without a logical, reasonable and unifying rationale. We should be able to perform this 'no'-delivering task with the receiver of the 'no' feeling they have been heard, understood and enlightened to a sensible ordering of organizational resource and priority.

People, however, are inherently selfish (ourselves included). This begins in humankind with the most basic of human traits relating to survival – people will naturally prioritize their *own* shelter, warmth and food over all others. This is the natural (and acceptable) root of our inherent selfishness. Unfortunately, in this case, roots tend to grow shoots, which in turn lead to branches. In our roles, we will eternally be plagued by the impact of this selfish human behaviour. An endless stream of 'Can I have a minute?' requests are waiting with each day to detract from our good and honest intentions. In practice these smaller regular distractions can be dealt with easily, the power of tomorrow will deal with them. Come back tomorrow, book some time in my diary and we will chat it through. A high percentage of the 'Can I have a minute?' brigade can be adequately dispatched with this technique. Or, by applying the long grass approach learned in Chapter 10.

It is the bigger fish who will cause us a real problem in this area of saying 'no', the senior leaders or directors who demand attention and may well be our primary customers. I am sure this point will bring vivid memories to mind for most experienced HR business partners. Saying 'no' to someone who owns a company or runs a major part of it can at times be more nuanced. I cannot set out a definitive answer for how to deal with all people, at all levels and at all times on this matter of saying 'no'. Suffice to say shrewd judgement is regularly required, and I would also advocate for the avoidance of absolutes – there should be nobody whom we *always* or *never* say 'no' to. If we are truly competent, then by the measure of the earlier definition, even directors will be on the receiving end of a 'no' from time to time.

The key point is this, many things and many people will seek to distract us at every turn. This is the nature of working in the business of people. People themselves, and people-related events, can sometimes be hard to predict. There is always an unforeseen element borne out of the individual characteristics and nature of the people involved in a situation or circumstance. It is these unforeseen elements that are most likely to derail us from our desired activity at any given moment. Ironically, knowing that these unforeseen moments are likely to spring up at any time should help us to plan for them. We cannot be completely surprised if we are pre-programmed to expect some human factor to interrupt us at an inconvenient moment. This prior knowledge and awareness will help us to continue to stay focused and stand firm in the face of the many people who are inadvertently seeking to throw us off our certain course.

From service provider to service designer

Therefore, to successfully travel the road to strategic, we must delicately traverse the path to progress from purely service provider, to service designer.

A service provider delivers a pre-defined service or set of services within predetermined boundaries or parameters. The terms are set for them and they must abide by those pre-set terms. There is always some room for influencing of the method of service provision, but largely, the 'what' of the service provision cannot be deviated from.

THE TWO EXTREMES OF SERVICE PROVISION

This is not a conclusive definition of the service provider. I must remind you again that I am prone to exaggerate for effect if I believe it will bring someone closer to understanding a truth.

To illustrate this point, I will state here that the service provision is hard to influence or change, whereas elsewhere I will campaign for, and unpack how, we can and should influence the provision of the service. By making this statement on service providers I do not mean to undermine the whole of Part Two, 'The people fundamentals', as it is that part that deals with 'how' a set of fixed services should be provided. In my experience and opinion, a service-providing HR business partner who does not understand any of the people fundamentals is offering a fundamentally different service to one who has mastered the people fundamentals.

So, in my mind those two extremes of service provision are so different as to become two entirely different service offerings, one far more desirable than the other. And, I would expect that mastering the people fundamentals will quickly lead down the track towards service designer in any case.

A service designer is someone who has implicit or explicit permission to lead on the creation of effective solutions, being fully cognizant of all relevant factors, to design and deliver comprehensive, restorative and deliverable services. Another hallmark of the service designer is their ability to complete large parts of this task autonomously, almost as if they already know the business well enough to also know what it needs. They are likely to be an insider. This is where the importance of Chapter 2, 'Knowing the business', comes to the fore.

If you are already a proven and successful service designer, you may have achieved this success by being focused on key goals and avoiding distractions that would have otherwise prevented such achievement, or the process of achievement will have provided you with a platform of trust from which to say 'no'. Either way, the outcome should create the required opportunity to develop our service offerings into this service designer territory.

This is a key component of the case for saying 'no'. As we have already discussed, there must be a credible reason on which to hang the 'no'. 'No' on its own is just plain insubordination.

Do not let yourself be distracted

On the road to strategic, we must be in the habit of creating and protecting both our own and the organization's capacity. The effective deployment of 'no' will be a frequently used tool in this noble quest for a higher goal.

'Say no to strangers' should be a rallying cry and a constant reminder to stay focused, stay on course, and not be blown off by the events of the day, week, month or year. Saying 'no' in this context is to ensure that the increasingly more strategic-minded HR business partner has clarity of vision to see the bigger picture and develop people strategies, which ultimately deliver on organizational goals.

Single-mindedness to the true cause will require us to periodically say 'no' and 'because'. Each day there are many people who need reminding of what was rigorously tested, proven and agreed only the day before. A commitment to the correct plan and an effective use of the word 'no', will see us deliver real and lasting results.

Summary

To begin with, the idea of saying no to strangers is about avoiding certain types of undesirable activity that will take us away from our goal of delivering strategic-level solutions. In order to be strategic we must first create the required headroom to give us the bandwidth we need. We are required to be conscientious in this matter of what work we put off or refuse to do. We need to learn *when* to say no. Sometimes there will be no consequences when you stop performing a task. Other times though, saying no will come with additional pressure to consistently perform at a high level in the tasks we do take on. In order to stay focused on the performance of strategic activity we need to hone our ability to explain why we are saying no. Our 'no' should always be accompanied by a 'because'. In preparing to become strategic we will transition from a purely service provider, to a more nuanced service designer. A service designer can create effective solutions that deliver comprehensive and restorative services. To become an effective service designer we will need to look to shed some of the less complex activity on our slate. This is how we create personal and organizational capacity. This capacity can then be used to tackle the complex strategic-level problems that threaten the businesses we serve.

Next, we will look at the final principle in this section on the road to strategic – being a pragmatist.

References

BFI (2021) *Say No to Strangers*, film [online] www.bfi.org.uk/films-tv-people/4ce2b79d5693e (archived at https://perma.cc/3TBX-3LX8)

Brooklyn Nine-Nine Site (2015–2020) The bank job, *Brooklyn Nine-Nine*, season 4, episode 21, aired 23 May 2017 [online] https://theninenine.com/quotes/episode/421/The-Bank-Job/src=epg/ (archived at https://perma.cc/E95N-8AHP)

12

Ever the pragmatist

A behaviour change

We are still on the road to strategic; we are altering what has been to prepare ourselves for what we must do next. Becoming strategic is a journey not a job title, and therefore we need to prepare ourselves for the journey and choose our route carefully.

In Chapters 10 and 11 we have focused on principles that help us to make space. This extra space is necessary to enable us to take on new strategic-level activity. These two chapters have hopefully created the clearing in the wilderness referred to at the beginning of Part Three.

It is now time to consider how we adapt to meet the challenge of becoming strategic. We must recognize that the things that have gotten us this far may not carry us all the way. Some learned behaviours will have to change. The interpretation and eloquent communication of complex rules and issues will not be enough on its own to enable us to become strategic. Until now you may have had a rules-based approach, especially if your background has been in HR advisory or transactional tasks. This chapter signals a behaviour modification that we will need to perform if we are going to be ready to take on the role of service designer and arrive successfully at our strategic destination.

An unfortunate truth

I use the phrase 'ever the pragmatist' to refer to myself on a regular basis, both out loud and in my head. I probably think it far more often than I speak it. On first hearing, this phrase may sound defeatist or compromising of our earlier principles, but the longer and deeper we get into the business of people the more essential this principle will become in creating successful outcomes.

We will, in the business of people, at some point have to navigate between the principle of 'playing a straight bat' and the objective of 'doing the right thing' or getting the right outcome. I have referred to this previously as the difference between the correct answer and the right solution. This morally courageous approach of 'playing a straight bat', in matters of people, will not always yield something that we can all agree on as the right outcome. I have frequently found this to be an unfortunate truth.

This is a potentially unpopular idea as it conflicts with some commonly held views. Implicitly, within parts of the HR profession there is an applied belief that consistently operating our policies and processes in the pursuit of 'fairness' will mean that our work, and therefore role, will be legitimized. As with all things related to people, life is unfortunately never that simple.

There is a deep paradox occurring in this subject. One of the predominant features of HR business partners is that we can be counted on to discharge the uniform corporate lines in the pursuit of fairness and consistency. But what should be done when it can be foreseen that to apply the consistent approach will bring about a wrong, or undesirable, outcome. How do our weighing scales balance, or sense of right and wrong be upheld, when all about us, and we ourselves, *feel* that the proposed outcome is the wrong one?

The means or the end

It seems sensible to attempt to explore this problem through the lens of a closely related and well-understood dilemma:

Does the means justify the end, or does the end justify the means?

The first relevant question for us to ask, in response to this dilemma, is this: should we adopt a principled position and apply either of these approaches, means or end, absolutely? I believe the answer to be no. A well-reasoned, principled decision for exclusively applying only means or end is sure to, at some point, be seen to be tantamount to bloody-mindedness by someone somewhere. This usually manifests as principles for principles sake, the means justifying the means. As we will find, this would also be out of kilter with this principle of ever the pragmatist.

This dilemma of means versus end is an often-painful reality for us as HR business partners operating in the business of people. We will test out both options, means and end, in a range of differing circumstances across lengthy reference periods of many years, only to discover that sage judgement, and a penchant for accurately predicting the future, is ultimately more effective than a decision solely based on means or end. Perhaps this is where we really learn critical thinking, perhaps this is really what 'added value' in action looks like – foresight and sage judgement. Those two qualities unequivocally add value in the business of people.

I find that the second relevant question to ask is: should we direct situations and circumstances in pursuit of a means or an end approach being achieved? By this I mean, in the process of making decisions that will have a direct impact and effect on people, should we uphold the process, or should we instead prioritize the outcome if the process won't provide the right solution? This is the eternal question with which HR business partners are made to wrestle.

If we could always exclusively pre-judge any dynamic set of circumstances involving people, how they will think and feel, to arrive at an outcome that everyone agrees is 'right', or the 'best' outcome, or 'fair' to those involved, then we would be able to discern between means and end as the correct approach. However, we all know that the world does not work that way, and that predicting how people will think and feel and what they need at any given moment can be somewhat fluid. People are not mathematics. Clear answers do not always exist.

In terms of our HR wiring, many of us have been pre-conditioned to favour 'means' approaches. Remembering the behaviour change that is required here for us to become strategic, we need to train ourselves to see the end. An eye on the end helps us to consider whether the means approach is entirely appropriate. This action is the seed of the behaviour change we are seeking. Whilst an exclusive in-principle approach that favours end would be wrong, there will surely be times when it is conscientious to ditch the means and plump for an end justification.

Ultimately, we should relieve ourselves from the responsibility of discovering the absolute answer to means versus end. Instead, we must be fully cognizant of both approaches at work explicitly and implicitly in the business of people. This awareness of the problem can be used to make informed decisions that are not ignorant of this dilemma.

A depth of experience in this area will often bring about some wisdom that will help to more accurately assess these difficult circumstances, in achieving good, right and fair outcomes and solutions. This wisdom is one of the hallmarks of the people-expert.

Embodying the pragmatist

Means and end is a complicated debate that will always create at least two opposite or opposing sides, and is one which will not necessarily be solved to the satisfaction of either. So, to develop our thinking in this area, and hopefully offer practical solutions on which we can all agree, we will return to the title of this chapter, 'ever the pragmatist'.

As has hopefully been noted by now, I try to be careful with my words and I am intentional with the words I choose to use. I find that this is a prudent trait for an HR business partner. Therefore, to illustrate this point, the title of this chapter is not 'being pragmatic', or 'taking a pragmatic approach'. Those are examples of things that can be picked up and put down; they are useful options or tactics to be used from time-to-time. Instead, this chapter is titled 'ever', as in 'always', 'the pragmatist', as in 'a person who is guided more by practical considerations than by ideals' (Oxford Languages, 2021).

So, rather than having to solve the never-ending means or end dilemma, this principle gives us a totally different pitch on which to play. Personally, this is a go-to strategy for me in all aspects of working life. If I do not like the options presented, I will seek to change the game so that I might have some different options that are more palatable to me. As I will explain in Chapter 13, I usually refer to this as divergent thinking. Put simply, how can we think about this problem in a different way, such that it brings about a different set of options or routes to success. I would rather attempt this difficult task than opt for an undesirable option.

Generally speaking, the HR function will generate strategy, policy, practice and processes based on 'ideals'. Ideals means ideal scenarios or generic circumstances, often to the exclusion of any complicating factors. This is what the HR function should be doing, there is no time, or corporate requirement, to tailor everything to everyone on every occasion or for every possible scenario. Instead, broad-brush ideals are created, and the people of the business are required to fall in line with these principles that are built for ideal circumstances. This approach will work just fine for the HR function at large, but what about for the HR business partner who must deliver these into local business areas?

Anyone who has been in the role for more than a few days will know that not every well-meaning idea, or thought, can be applied perfectly in the real world. This becomes one of our major sufferings as HR business partners that seems destined to repeat itself with a never-ending nauseating cycle of spiralling doom. The repeatedly occurring problem is this: HR business partners are perpetually asked to implement interventions, systems, processes or points of policy, which are created behind closed doors in little dark rooms with reference to no-one's real-world experience.

If you are not sure what I am referring to here let me assure you that unfortunately this really can happen. I once heard of a particularly overbearing organizational development team who had one of these little dark rooms. First, they had the glass walls frosted over so no one could see in, then they proceeded to seemingly cover the entire room from head-to-toe in post-it notes and flipchart paper. In a break from organizational culture, this room became the only lockable meeting room in a large three-storey building. I guess if you will lock yourself away from the world you really do lose your grip on reality.

This description of little dark rooms might sound harsh (and as I have said already, I am prone to exaggerate for effect), but it turns out there is a huge chasm between good ideas and ideas that work well in practice. Whilst this is a perpetual problem it may not be a frequently occurring one. Hopefully these instances are few and far between. Over time I have been frustrated with this corporate practice of producing impractical or unworkable ideas. Personally, I have started to refer to these unsuitable initiatives as 'nice ideas'. Using the word 'nice' as an adjective in this context seems to appropriately convey a professional level of disdain without unduly upsetting anyone. As in, 'it is a nice idea, but it will never work'.

Corporately created ideas can often be good for the whole but unimplementable for individual business areas. These interventions cause our business areas to recoil from the table in horror at what the HR function is asking them to do in the name of corporate obedience. It is then our role to bridge the gap again between the diktat from HR and the ongoing wants and needs of the business. Inevitably this will involve us moving HR closer to the business's requests or the business closer to HR's (often the latter).

Therefore, we must become adept at recognizing and distinguishing between good ideas and practicably workable ideas. We cannot assume that ideas are always both good and practically workable. Having knowledge of the business and an orientation for adding value will enable us to develop this skill for spotting the practical from the good.

The stupid idea

Before we jump down the throat of this controversial subject of stupid ideas, I must provide a health warning. It may sound unprofessional to call something in business 'stupid', especially in print, but having attempted to seek an alternative word I can assure you this is the correct description of what we are talking about here. Firstly, please treat the use of this word with the semi-jovial nature intended. Secondly, given where we are on our journey, I am assuming that I am talking to a highly developed HR business partner who might by now have formed some strong and clear opinions on what is good and right in the business of people. This experiential wisdom will enable us to assess when an HR initiative is good, elegant and clever. Conversely, this knowledge will mean there are times when our assessment of a thing concludes that it is poor, clumsy or indeed stupid.

Hopefully for most, discernment of ideas will end at the sifting between the practical and the good. However, I have found that some circumstances require additional antennae to assess a deeper and more grievous product of little-dark-room thinking: the stupid idea.

We do not want to be seen to be going around and knocking down other people's genuine attempts at good work; however, it is important to be aware of ideas that really are a little too stupid to be given more bandwidth than is necessary. Perfectly good and well-meaning people can, sometimes, arrive at ill-conceived and impractical solutions that, were they to be implemented, qualify as stupid. It is a foible of being human. We should understand that it is not the person who is stupid, or being stupid, it is just the idea that is stupid. When being creative, people should be given wide latitude to make mistakes of creation; however, there is no excuse for mistakes of application. People should be encouraged, but ideas should be critically tested.

The problem is what happens when this stupid idea comes towards us over the fence or emerges from the depths of the little dark room. If the idea is from within the HR function it will commonly land in the lap of the HR business partner for implementing. This means that we then have a decision to make: how to approach the implementation of a stupid idea. The *other* decision is usually untenable. I would not advise refusing to implement something that was given to us to do as part of our duties. Instead of refusal, influence should be used to amend or alter the idea to make it less stupid. If that fails, then only pragmatism will do.

The main concern for us here is being seen to champion or push forward a scheme that does not translate well in the business and is likely to fail. None of us want to find ourselves in that position because it will adversely affect our credibility. We have been carefully and deliberately tending to the building of trust and credibility throughout our journey. Let us remember that we highly value our delicately built trust and credibility and are unlikely to risk it, unless it is to stand against an injustice or an outrage.

The bridge over this divide then must be the pragmatist. Someone who is more concerned with the practical considerations as well as their own and the HR function's credibility, will be able to coordinate the needs of all parties to reach a solution that is both workable and sensible in the circumstances. It takes the HR business partner to embody the role of the pragmatist to ensure neither HR nor the business feels compromised, yet each leaves happier than they came.

To complete this bridge analogy, we should look at the component parts of a bridge to effectively visualize our pragmatist role between HR and the business. As set out in Figure 12.1, the HR business partner girders sits across the HR and business abutments at opposite sides of the bridge. Our piles are rooted deep in trust and credibility, causing our foundation to be firm. Our piers are capped with the knowledge of HR, knowledge of the business and adding value. Finally, our load-bearing girders are constructed from pure HR business partner pragmatism.

FIGURE 12.1   The HR business partner pragmatist bridge

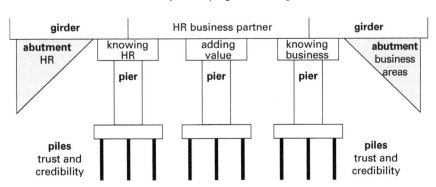

SOURCE Glenn Templeman (2021)

Adopting the mind and positional status of a pragmatist is the remedy to treat these stupid ideas. In the HR business partner, stupid ideas are tweaked, iterated, amended and improved to meet the many practical considerations that are essential to successful, effective and workable solutions.

Resolving our differences

So, if the HR function at large is guided by ideals, and we are guided more by practical considerations, how will this difference be resolved?

Ultimately, we are guided *more*, but not exclusively, by practical considerations than ideals. This means that we can and will continue to uphold the principles of fairness through the application of ideally formed strategy, policy and process. To be guided exclusively by practical considerations would be complete anarchy. No decision would have any consistency at all except by coincidence. Everyone would get exactly what they want all the time, and of course (as we should already have learned by now), if everyone wins, no one wins. However, the simple fact remains, not everything constructed by the HR function will always work perfectly in practice. We cannot always do everything the HR function asks of us, on every occasion, in the way that it is requested to be done. This is not insubordination, it is pragmatism in action. Perhaps this is or will in future be the justification for replacing us with artificial intelligence or robots!

In these situations, our role is to blend the ideals with the real-world practical implications to reach a good, sensible and reasonable outcome for all, ensuring that no one, including ourselves, feels too gravely compromised. As a matter of fact, this is probably a pithy aphorism of the role of the HR business partner, applicable to almost every situation we will find ourselves.

Well-managed compromise has the strange and counter-intuitive effect of building trust and creating credibility. For a role so steeped in morals and principles, you would think that regular compromise and individual deal-making would adversely affect one's credibility and the building of trust. However, when these compromises are pursued in the spirit of a genuine desire to achieve the best and fair outcome for everyone, compromise seems to become an honourable act. I think it must be because there is great power in the ability to see each person's need and understand them individually, so that a breaking of convention, or compromise, is perceived as true power exercised courageously for the benefit of those affected.

Of course, there is a balance to be struck between principles and compromise, and there are sure to be some 'red lines' and limits to how many, or how often, principles can be bent or broken to bow to compromise. We can and should fall back on our policies and processes when we need them to bring about order at the right time.

There comes a point where pure pragmatism must prevail – whether principled or compromising, we will come to appreciate that we cannot please all the people *any* of the time.

Next stop strategic

This is the last stop on the journey before we arrive at our long-awaited strategic destination. It is important that we consider the behaviour modification of pragmatism before we arrive at Part Four, 'The clever stuff'. Throughout we have been seeking not to simply change what we do but also how we think. Changing how we think is much more effective than taking on new tasks. Again, here we will need to think differently to embrace pragmatism before we dive headfirst into the strategic realm. Failing to understand the balance between principles and compromise will leave us all at sea in the new strategic world.

Ever the pragmatist should teach us to discern the right action in every circumstance. Knowing we are the pragmatist in the equation should orientate us to be the mediator and deal-maker as and when required. Thinking of ourselves and our role in this way will put us in the right position to be able to operate effectively in the strategic realm. Strategy must be commenced from the right position; the pragmatist will help us to embrace this position. The pragmatist is an important skill for us to learn and hone before we move on to strategic service design for our business.

Summary

In summary, ever the pragmatist means that some of our previous behaviour may have to change, especially if we have been used to a rules-based approach. The pragmatist comes into its own in the business of people where giving the correct answer is in conflict with doing the right thing. There are times where the organizational policies and processes that are designed to ensure 'fairness' fall short of that aim. In these cases, an intermediary pragmatist will be required. On this point of ensuring fairness, we will have to consider whether the means justifies the end or vice versa. Typically, the HR function have favoured means approaches and the HR business partner will have to be cognizant of this when designing and delivering effective end-justified solutions. This will require us to embody the pragmatist and be a person who is guided more by practical considerations than by ideals. Problems arise for us when corporately created ideas are designed without enough reference to individual business needs. Therefore, we must become adept at recognizing and distinguishing ideas that are practicably workable. Our experiential wisdom will enable us to assess when an initiative is good, elegant and clever. Conversely, this knowledge will mean that we know when something is doomed to fail. This people-expert experience will protect everyone from so-called stupid ideas. Our role is to blend ideals with real-world practical implications to reach good, sensible and reasonable outcomes for all, ensuring that no one feels too compromised in the process. This is pragmatism in action.

This was the final stop on our road to strategic. Next, we move onto Part Four, 'The clever stuff'!

Reference

Oxford Languages (2021) Pragmatist, *Oxford English Dictionary*, Oxford University Press

The clever stuff

We have finally arrived at 'The clever stuff' after having travelled carefully via 'The road to strategic'. 'Our foundational structure' and 'People fundamentals' still hold true and provide us with the firm base on which to begin to add clever stuff.

As is hopefully clear by this point, Part Four will focus on the strategic elements of HR business partnering. This has been our destination throughout, and I aim in this section to unpack the key elements of how to think like a strategic-service-designing people-expert HR business partner. The elements of this section are few but individually and collectively are deep in value and significance.

Becoming a strategic-level HR business partner is nine-tenths preparatory. Most of the hard work is done in building the correct foundations from which to leverage strategic people offerings. Therefore, the structure of this book is heavily weighted towards the foundational fundamentals that we have already considered. I believe it is difficult for us to operate successfully at the strategic level without first having some active grasp and successful application of the preceding 12 chapters.

Much of our foundations and fundamentals are based in common sense and good logic, the value of which is easily appreciated for what it is. Viewpoints can become much murkier when it comes to the creation and application of strategy. The word 'strategy' has been banded around so liberally that over time it has become something of an amorphous blob of random and unrelated things. This is an unfortunate setting for an often poorly understood subject.

The problem for the average HR business partner is that the generalist nature of our role is so broad that it can be a very tall order to master everything we have already discussed and add these upcoming strategic elements. I believe it to be true that everything we have discussed to this point is within our gift to master. However, adding these deep strategic skills is perhaps something never to be fully mastered but instead it is to be continually learnt and practised. There are experts out there who could perhaps claim to have mastered all this clever stuff, but none of these experts are likely to have also mastered all the preceding principles in our book. We, on the other hand, are seeking to sustain our status as generalists, a fact that should not be forgotten when we are adding strategic abilities.

Making the transition into a strategic-focused HR role is the biggest existential challenge we are likely to face in our career. Many have made the transition but often the difference is in name only.

I will aim here to bring us some tracks on which to reset our strategy train.

13

Strategic is a mindset

The strategy disarray

Within the HR profession we put a lot of emphasis on ensuring we are offering businesses strategic services and offerings. This is a right and noble cause with the best of intentions. However, there is always a big gap between intention and destination. It is the HR business partner that often finds themselves standing directly in this big gap. This creates the case for us to lead the charge on the delivery of strategic activity. In order to achieve this successfully, we must first be in our right minds on this subject of strategy.

To those who are not familiar with the world of strategy or who do not understand it well, it is often littered with vague overtones, opaque gestures, deeply tenuous links and classical clichés. These features are not useful for our purposes. Sometimes it can seem that no one really knows what they, or anyone else in the room, are talking about. Strategy-land really can be a very confusing and mysterious place at times.

This mystery and confusion are often compounded in the HR function when we add in two additional factors: 1) the subject of our strategy musings is an even more amorphous blob – people; and 2) the HR business partner has their title amended with the prefix of 'Strategic', to encourage their magical transformation into a lofty new strategic being.

It appears the only thing more confusing than devising and implementing strategy is the action of 'being strategic'. It seems right that I should briefly pause on this statement and point out the obvious – not all of us struggle with operating strategically, or 'being strategic'. There are many talented people who have mastered this strategic paradigm. Although it does seem that many of them move on from senior HR business partner roles into more senior head of HR or HR director type roles (more on this in Chapter 17). However, in my experience I have found that many do indeed struggle. It is one of my main motivations for writing this book. Over many years I have continuously encountered senior-level HR business partners who are abdicating their strategic responsibilities due to a lack of knowledge or experience, or both, in how to go about 'being strategic'.

This challenge of 'being strategic' affects the entire HR profession and touches every role within our HR functions. However, rather than precisely understanding how every role within the function contributes to the delivery of strategic activity, we seem to have instead created a profession-wide hierarchy that places the strategic activity only with the most senior of HR business partners.

This creates a kind of strategy pressure cooker – a model that requires our most senior practitioners to perform strategic magic tricks whilst the rest of the function, and the business, is eagerly watching and waiting to be entertained. It should not come as a surprise that solving strategic problems with job title prefixes is not a model which tends to work that well.

For a profession that has since the late 1990s sought to move the needle in terms of offerings and perception, it seems odd that we have somehow ended up with an expectation that there be only one role that must perform all these wonderfully whizz-bang strategic interventions. Why wouldn't we seek to embed this strategic operation at all levels throughout the function? What if there were a way to do this without upsetting the hierarchical equilibrium of the status quo?

Maybe these are all ambitious questions, but if we start to think of flatter structures with delegated decision making it might just become an achievable idea. Especially if we also give people the explicit permission to think independently.

Again, on this idea of where the strategic onus sits, I am exaggerating and generalizing for effect here to make the point for us – there won't just be the one role within the HR function with a strategic remit. Obviously, at least the HR director and the rest of the HR leadership team will be operating strategically too. But from a functional practitioner level, the HR business partner is often lonely within the HR function when operating in the strategic realm.

No one has the monopoly on thought

Rather than trying to dig into all the things that are wrong with the way we often consider strategy in the business of people, I want to instead focus on how we should approach strategic things. We should focus on that which is in our control. As the chapter title suggests, I wish to propagate a clear approach to the consideration of the phrase 'strategic', an approach that can be applied by anyone at any level within the HR function. The great thing about a mindset is that it is not exclusive, no one can be left out of a way of thinking if they choose to think that way. If we allow all our people to think independently, and those who wish to can consider strategic things irrespective of their current position in the hierarchy, we might just start a revolution.

WHAT STRATEGIC IS NOT

Remember: Strategic is a mindset. It is not: a hierarchy, a job title, a workstream, a framework, a team or a role.

Of course, we frequently articulate strategy in one or all of those terms, but in order to successfully traverse this strategic hurdle, it is important to reset our thinking on this subject. I can confirm that cultivating a strategic mindset is far more effective than seeking to act in a strategic way. We need to think before we act. As I have explained previously, there is a great deal of benefit to be gained by taking the time to think and consider a subject, and in this case, thinking is usually preferable to doing, especially if 'being strategic' is a new pastime for you.

In fact, those who opt for doing over thinking in this strategic sphere often seem to drift aimlessly back to exactly whatever they were doing before someone suggested that they 'become strategic'.

To illustrate this point, in general terms I have met perhaps four types of HR business partners who appear to reside in this strategic realm: 1) those who get it and are already off changing the world for the better; 2) those who struggle with the broad remit of being strategic but have nevertheless mastered a niche or specialism that masks their lack of strategic breadth; 3) those who seem to have enough acumen to understand they should be doing something different but simply and consciously choose not to engage with this idea of being strategic; and 4) those who never admit that they have absolutely no clue what is meant by the term strategic and carry on blindly with other seemingly more important tasks. Some people can even flit in and out of more than one category simultaneously.

So, my rather reductive assessment of the strategic HR business partner problem indicates, I believe, that mindset plays a big part in the successful application of this strategic concept. There is a good deal of thought by everyone in the first three categories (whether it be positive or negative thought), and a complete lack of thought by those occupying the final category. Therefore, thought, or lack thereof, is a central and essential theme across all four categories. The underlying assumption is that the people in the first category have been able to harness strategic activity because they have acquired the corresponding mindset to facilitate it. The absence of the right mindset in the other three groups has the effect of causing them to fall short.

If we embrace this idea that the battle for strategic is won and lost in the mind, we can break free of constraining strategic thinking to just the most senior HR folk. Then everyone in the HR function can be allowed to also begin to think strategically. Spreading the expectation will lower the temperature in the strategic HR business partner pressure cooker.

Relieving strategic HR business partners from the expectation of being the sole HR proponent of strategic people things provides two key benefits for the HR profession and the business: 1) others start to see what we see, which creates a band of HR advocates seeking right solutions (as opposed to correct answers); and 2) rather than the four types of strategic HR business partner listed earlier, more often than not this approach will generate type one people – 'those who get it' and will change the world for the better.

Rather than seeking out diversionary tactics, if we are set firm in our foundations and fundamentals, we can then set our *minds* on what it means to be strategic. Applying this approach will lead to more strategic thought leaders rising to provide examples that the whole HR function can follow.

If we can treat these problems through the altering and acquiring of specific thinking, simultaneously turning these trails of thought into a totality we can call a mindset, then we might just have some profession-altering progress in the pipeline.

The art of perpetual thinking

So how does one begin thinking strategically and adopting this practice as a mindset?

We have already discussed the benefit of carving out time that can be dedicated to directed thinking on a subject. However, in this case we are not trying to think specifically about a thing, we are instead trying to develop and hone a *way* of thinking. This means we need to start practising thinking in this way all the time about all things. 'All the time', is of course the best way to practise anything that one wants to get good at. We should consider this term *thinking* as something we do that is continuous and never ceasing, with a kind of imperative urgency. This continuous stream of thinking is the necessary first step in developing a strategic mindset. It is a practice that will prepare the mind to begin to assess the situations we see around us every day.

The careful reader will notice that we are talking about a way of thinking and that I have suggested thinking continuously but not exactly mentioned what to think about just yet! This approach is in treatment of a specific root cause that is prevalent amongst busy HR business partners, that is – a lack of thinking. It is common, especially once we are well established in our position, for us to stop thinking anything new.

Busyness and the pursuit of efficiency take over and our thinking turns into processing. Specifically, I mean because of the continuous pressures of time there is just no room for any novel thought anymore. No opportunity is afforded to consider radical changes to the way everyday tasks are performed. Thinking and processing are not the same things. Processing is not a form of thinking by our earlier definition, even though it also takes place in the mind. Processing is to understand that when 'x' occurs, the solution is 'y'. That kind of autopilot assessment can be learnt, and remembered, so that it can be applied quickly at the appropriate moment, but for our purposes that is defined as processing, not thinking.

This kind of processing is not the thinking we are seeking to develop, it is instead providing answers based on things *already known*. To use a simplistic analogy, we could describe this as similar to the difference between a dictionary and a thesaurus. The role of the dictionary is to provide definitive answers to the meaning of a word; the thesaurus, however, must think differently about the definition of the chosen word to provide an alternative range of answers to the same question. A subtle but definite difference.

The provision of answers based on things that are *already known* is clearly a function that could be delivered by a system or process, and perhaps instead by computers or robotics. Therefore, providing answers to things already known should be a practice for us humans to move away from, in favour of true value-add activity.

When we are permanently busy, we cut corners with the aim of increasing our output, this is a very natural and sometimes necessary behaviour and we can easily fall into this trap. In these instances, thinking is stopped in the pursuit of ultimate efficiency. This is what I would call a semi-conscious approach to stopping thinking in the pursuit of saving time. There is also a more acute scenario where time is *so* pressed that thinking is stopped to facilitate survival. This is a kind of unconscious and desperate approach to achieving one's tasks in the allotted time frame, or lack thereof. Moving at this sort of pace usually creates a high propensity for errors to occur. We should keep this risk in mind when we are at our busiest.

Therefore, the first step in creating a strategic mindset is to learn to think again. We should do this by practising thinking as an ongoing obligation of our presence within a business. Every time we are observing people, we should be initiating this type of active applied thinking.

This thinking habit will become a two-part exercise. We have already covered the first part, which is to train the mind to think continuously, and then use this to objectively assess the current people, circumstances and relevant factors within a business. With our genuine interest in people as a prerequisite, this type of thinking should come naturally. This type of analytical thought about the business's people is required for the second part of the exercise: recognizing patterns.

This new skill of continuous thought is applied in the form of recognizing similarities between issues and reoccurring themes, seeking out patterns and synergies in the problems we see each day.

Spotting people patterns

We have already set the stage to be the people-expert, the human in the machine who is chiefly concerned with one thing, namely people. This holistic approach to the business of people must now be applied to the art of our thought too. As I have already alluded to, it is tricky to develop a strategic mindset in the subject of people, without a genuine interest in people. This genuine interest in people is a quality to keep in mind when looking to spot patterns and understand what to do with those patterns when we find them.

We should apply continuous thought to recognise consistencies and patterns, and then synthesize them into coherent and recognizable common problem statements.

This is a kind of analytical filtration process to sift through all the different pieces of the jigsaw puzzle. Except that there are pieces from at least a dozen different jigsaw puzzles and some of the individual pieces will fit more than one of the dozen different puzzles. People are complex creatures, so when it comes to issues that cause problems, the problems can often be caused by a culmination of issues and not just one single issue. Whereas conversely, there will be separate instances where people problems will have been caused by one isolated issue. That is the problem with people, they always seem to sit in more than one box simultaneously. An individual's thoughts and feelings make it hard to package them neatly into one box.

Nevertheless, we need to sift through all this information on the commonly occurring people problems that surround us each day. This is where our genuine interest in people will make the process easier. In this sense, a 'genuine interest in people' means that we will have an *interest* in making things better for people. A natural goal of improving the working lives of others.

Being able to connect the dots between different people-related events, and draw straight lines between things that are causing confusion within a business and its people, is one of the most insightful things we can do.

The sifting and synthesizing of problems into coherent groups is to service the final part of the strategic mindset – the creation of strategic-level solutions.

Strategic solutions fit for strategic problems

Solving individual people problems on a case-by-case basis is unlikely to be in step with the exercising of a strategic mindset. As discussed already, dealing with problems one by one, as and when they arise, is more akin to processing than the thinking we are seeking to attain.

To develop a strategic mindset, this type of continuous thought must assess and sort problems into high-level groupings to allow for strategic-level solutions to be devised. The commonality of issues must be assessed so that the determined grouping can be treated by a correspondingly significant level of solution. To use an illustration from our world, we would not address a proven case of gross misconduct with a 30-minute online training course. Nor should we attempt to deal with the symptoms of wide-ranging systemic issues with basic or binary solutions.

This then is the beginning of the fun part. Having done the tough and diligent tasks required by continuous thought and synthetization of disparate data points, we reach the moment in the strategic mindset challenge of creating suitable solutions.

Arrival at the solution point of this mindset approach emphasizes the importance of creating solid, coherent, sensible and logical problem statements. If the problem statements are fanciful or inaccurate, then the corresponding solutions are sure to be way offbeat. Offbeat solutions will do nothing for building trust and credibility in HR business partners or the HR function.

For the solutions to be solid, the problem statements must first be dependable. A large part of landing on dependable problem statements will be the input and understanding of others. If a problem statement is solid, it should take very little time and convincing for someone else familiar with the matter to agree with its principles. Once conceived, we should look to socialize and test these draft problem statements with other relevant and trustworthy people. This is easily achieved through the medium of everyday conversation in the course of our normal duties.

Once the solid problem statements are confirmed, we can turn our mind to strategic-level solutions.

The highest common factor

The logic here is that somehow in banding the problems together and looking for the highest common factor or the key thread that runs through all problems, we will be able to address solutions at an overarching strategic level, instead of considering each problem in isolation. Ergo, great many groups of problems can be solved simultaneously by a single high-level overarching strategic solution. Elevating our thought to the highest common factor enables us to define solutions that will address the core root issues.

Processes deal with one thing at a time, policies deal with most things most of the time, but strategy deals with everything all the time. This is because strategic-level interventions provide the pitch on which the game is to be played, good strategy brings order to all else. Strategy is the umbrella that covers everything – when it is dry outside the people stay dry, when it rains the people are still dry. This is the power of effective strategy.

It is impossible here to provide a range of potential problem statements and corresponding strategic-level solutions. However, to make clear what I am trying to explain, it will be beneficial to consider a hypothetical example:

We could, on any given day, encounter the following three seemingly unrelated issues: 1) a meeting where discussions appear circular and confused, which concludes without any clear actions or outcomes; 2) two different managers from the same business area adopting entirely different positions on a key issue; and 3) another HR business partner colleague who works with a different part of the business calling into question the value of the contribution of the business area cited in 1) and 2).

There could be many big-ticket items contributing to these individual problems; however, to adequately illustrate the highest common factor point let's keep things simple and say that there is one common problem statement that would cover all three of these issues. The common problem here could be that the business area in question has a lack of clear goals or has failed to adequately explain their goals to the people within the business area and to the wider organization.

In this example, the corresponding strategic-level solution is likely to revolve around reviewing the current business area goals to ensure they are clear and translatable to those who are inside and outside the business area, so that sufficient horizontal and vertical alignment can be achieved and understood by anyone in any position within the organization. The goals must be simple enough that people at all levels can understand them and see how they contribute to the overall aims of the organization.

IS IT A PEOPLE PROBLEM THOUGH?

You might be reading the example and think to yourself, 'this sounds like a problem for the business, not a problem for HR to solve'. If you were thinking that, you might be partly right. It is a business's problem to *own* but it is a problem that is manifesting in their people. This is exactly the type of problem that needs an HR business partner strategic solution.

In the case of this example, it will take a people-expert with knowledge of the business to effectively review and repackage these business area goals into ways that the people of the business will relate to and understand. This kind of added value is hard to express in facts and figures, but it has a very real effect on a business and its people.

Part of the challenge for us is not just spotting the patterns, coming up with strategic-level solutions and discerning the highest common factor, it is filtering what qualifies as a people problem in the first place. We will need to ask ourselves this question continuously when hearing of all problems, and especially those that are not initially presented to us as 'people' problems. Real value is added when we create strategic people solutions when others failed to realize that it was indeed a people problem.

This is the basis of a strategic-level solution. To consider this example from a different angle, a tactical-level solution would be to take the existing goals in their current flawed state and go around re-explaining them ad infinitum to every individual or team. In this case, the tactical approach is likely to require more effort and be less effective. It is an example where only an overarching strategic-level solution will do. This is not to say that once a strategic-level solution is decided upon that it could not also be underpinned by complementary tactical-level interventions that are in line with the strategic solution.

This example illustrates what is meant by the assessment and sifting of problems, so that they can be synthesized into common problem statements which can be tackled at the strategic level.

Limitless creativity

This area of developing strategic solutions is perhaps where we have the most licence for creativity. Typically, businesses do not require their HR business partners to be overly creative; there are many qualities required but creativity often falls lower down the wish lists of most businesses. The creation of strategic interventions is typically the purest moment of creativity within our wide-ranging remit.

Sometimes, this creative thinking is simply a case of connecting groups of problems to already available solutions. This is more than the $x = y$ of processing because the thinking still must be done to assess and group the problems. Inevitably there will be many nuances and barriers in making the leap from the group of problems to the ready-made solution. In this scenario there is more thinking involved than meets the eye.

More often, this creativity is required to create something that the business does not currently have and has perhaps not seen before. This is real professional creativity in action on our part. If the business area already knew the solution, they would *hopefully* already be implementing it themselves.

I like to think of this creativity in a purist sense – initially we should allow ourselves to think, without limitation, of solutions that would address the group of problems faced. Having initially considered any and all creative solutions (usually including sacking everyone and starting again), inside and outside the box as it were, thought can then be turned to versions of the unlimited solutions that are sensible and workable within the business to which they will be applied (remembering the principles of ever the pragmatist). This kind of expansive thought, beginning with the unlimited and coming back down to earth with the practical, will hopefully create the richest of strategic solutions. Whereas to limit oneself to purely practical solutions in the first instance is likely to create something far drabber and potentially less effective.

We must remember that we are well-positioned to undertake this kind of limitless creative thinking about a business's people problems. This is because we have already qualified as an expert in HR, the business itself and in adding value in the field of people. Therefore, we can be permitted this freedom to think creatively because we will always root our conclusions and solutions to the prevailing business and people circumstances. In this regard, we should be trusted to get it right, based on our prior knowledge and expertise.

Divergent solutions

This creation of something not before seen within a business will be a far easier task for those of us who *have* seen the solution before, albeit in a different business at another organization. Admittedly, this may be a harder task for those with no external business reference points on which to draw. However, this is where the wider profession plays a role; there are a wealth of professional publications, textbooks, training and resources available to us. Inquisitiveness and self-education are the tools of the progressive HR business partner. Nevertheless, to give some additional direction in this area of creative solutioning, I find there is one phrase that helps greatly – divergent thinking.

I will often talk about creating divergent solutions. I find that it is useful to introduce this phrase into conversations and use it to direct thinking because it specifically prefixes the potential solutions with the idea that they must be different or take a different direction. Use of the word therefore automatically disqualifies solutions that are not different to the status quo or which do not tend to lead in a different direction to the current approach.

At times this talk of *divergent* solutions can draw blank looks from all present, but being an HR business partner who is serious on the surface means that I am intentional with my words and I mean what I say. Perhaps the key takeaway here is that if others do not understand the words being used, then hopefully they will ask what they mean (which my colleagues frequently do) or go away and look those words up. Inquisitiveness is paramount at this strategic phase.

The idea of divergent thinking is that it can be used as a kind of test or check and balance by which to assess all possible solutions. If none are found to be sufficiently divergent then it should prompt us to think again, to think differently. Our attempt at creativity will have failed and we will need to redeem ourselves through a divergent route.

For those with little external reference to draw upon, the use of divergent thinking will hopefully act as a loyal aide in this quest for creativity of thought.

Practising strategic thinking

This subject of strategic thought is a difficult one to adequately explain in detail. Here I have attempted to lay out a system of linear thinking that I believe leads down the path to the development of a strategic mindset.

Some of these elements of linear thinking require additional input, which I have intentionally excluded from this chapter as we will address them in Chapters 14 and 15. Suffice to say we have laid the groundwork and frame for developing a strategic mindset to which we can now add these ideas of treatment and narrative. The strategic mindset comes first, once mastered we can then add more to enhance its effectiveness.

So, in short summary, we should begin this journey toward a strategic mindset through the development of continuous thought, the assessment and grouping of day-to-day people problems into high-level common problem statements, and then apply creativity in the development of sensible and practical solutions.

Practising this process of thought will hopefully lead to viewing the world around us in new and different ways. Each daily issue will cease to be a disconnected occurrence culminating in a groundhog day like feeling, and instead these frustrating events will become relevant data points in the validation of future viable solutions. Each occurrence will be assessed and tested for relevance and validity against our current working assumption set of common problem statements.

This process of continuous refinement of problem statements will enable us to continually create and adapt strategies that are effective in addressing and solving problems at the root cause.

A strategic mindset can do all this and more, it will ultimately improve our existence and the lives of all those surrounding us. Long-term cultivation of this strategic mindset is key, this will be no overnight sensation.

Summary

Strategy can be confusing and 'being strategic' can be even more baffling – especially when the subject matter is people! This challenge affects the entire HR profession and often creates pressure for the HR business partner to achieve this undefined strategic standard. Despite this pressure on the HR business partner, it is true that no one has the monopoly on thought. Therefore, developing a strategic mindset isn't limited by hierarchy, anyone is free to begin thinking in this way. Strategy is not a hierarchy, a job title, a workstream, a framework, a team or a role. It is a mindset. This means that the strategic battle is won and lost in the mind. To begin developing this mindset we need to master the art of perpetual thinking. To do this, we have to avoid the type of thinking about things already known (processing). Instead, we use the practice of continuous thinking to objectively assess circumstances relating to people within a business. Our genuine interest in people should enable this type of thought to come naturally. Then we will be able to begin recognizing patterns and turning them into coherent problem statements that others also understand. Once we have sifted and synthesized problems into coherent problem statements, we can then move onto create corresponding strategic-level solutions. This is where we pause to ensure our problem statements are solid. If the problem statements are inaccurate then the corresponding solutions are sure to miss the mark. We need to create strategic solutions that address the highest common factor or the key thread that runs through all the problems encountered. Aiming for the highest common factor ensures we don't attempt to address strategic-level problems with tactical-level solutions. Next, we can free our minds to think about solutions creatively without limit. Thought can then be turned to versions of the unlimited solutions that are sensible and workable within the business. This kind of expansive thought, beginning with the unlimited and coming back down to earth with the practical, will hopefully create the richest of strategic solutions. If, after this blast of creativity, we are still seeking strategic solutions, we can turn to divergent thinking to provide divergent solutions. Divergent thinking can be used to assess all possible solutions. If none are found to be sufficiently divergent then it should prompt us to think again, to think differently. Our attempt at strategic creativity will have failed and we will have to redeem ourselves through a divergent route.

The next chapter of 'The clever stuff' will take us onto a natural extension of the strategic mindset, avoiding treating symptoms and instead identifying and tackling root cause issues.

14

Don't treat the symptoms

Fruit from the root

Hot on the heels of a newly developed strategic mindset we should look to add complementary tools to continue to hone our ability to operate at the strategic level. These next two chapters are like fruit hanging from the branches of the strategic mindset tree. Therefore, this chapter is closely aligned with the previous one, 'Strategic is a mindset', to ensure we are building capability in an analogous and sustainable fashion.

Having embedded the strategic mindset we now need to ensure we apply the components of our strategic thinking to seek out and solve the *real* issue. A strategic mindset will be of little good if we cannot use it to successfully identify and solve people issues within our businesses.

Our intentions are undoubtedly upright when we attempt to operate in the strategic realm to identify and solve wide-ranging systemic people issues. However, we can often trip or fall, not because our intentions were wrong, or our knowledge incorrect, but because we attempted to solve the wrong issue. This mistake is easily made and will occur frequently in the business of people. It is common to attempt to solve what *seems* to be the issue. However, in this business of people, not everything is as it seems.

Our focus must then be exclusively on addressing root cause issues. Here we will discover how to define and discern these deceptive roots. Attempting to treat only the symptoms we see presenting is sure to give us trouble.

A more complex problem

In the modern world of business and organizational operations, life has gotten very busy indeed. We all have diaries full of daytime meetings and then we do the work arising from those meetings in the evenings. Many of us find ourselves time poor. It is generally accepted that most of us are trying to do too much with too little time, but we all continue to give it a pretty good go in any case!

Closely accompanying this very modern busyness is an appetite for oversimplifying the problems we encounter and, in so doing, reducing them down to digestible chunks that appear easily solved with puny solutions. I would usually advocate for any trend towards simplification, with one key exception being the pursuit of understanding people problems. In this instance we should not rush to simple conclusions. Too often there is a lack of appetite, presumably because of busyness (or occasionally laziness), to consider problems for what they really are, as opposed to what they may appear to be.

In practice this simplification and short-cutting involves identifying problems and knocking them down individually, which is commonly referred to as 'removing blockers', as if it were a misguided tactic in a sprint hurdle race. I believe this phrase is attributable to the programme management drumbeat that exists throughout the business world. I am happy, of course, to be corrected on that. Whatever it is attributable to, there is often a great deal of excitement and energy devoted to removing these 'blockers'. Unfortunately, in these scenarios, energy is directed in a blinkered, closed-minded way, without anyone taking the time to step back from these individual events to think about what would fix them *all* with one fell swoop. Still, at least the programmatic approach is living proof that some people are doing something... the term 'hurdles' also appears in the business lexicon. This is no coincidence I'm sure.

These two factors combined, the busyness and the penchant for tackling oversimplified and misdiagnosed individual issues as they arise, is essentially a tactical approach, not a strategic one, which can prove to be deeply inefficient when attempting to address systemic people issues.

There are circumstances, programmes and projects, where dealing with issues tactically is a proportionate method of achieving success; however, in the business of people, this is a sure-fire route to nowhere. It is tantamount to treading treacle. If we take on a mindset of 'knocking down blockers' as and when they arise, we will likely still be dealing with Monday morning's problems on Friday night. People-rooted issues are usually more complex than that. We must have a better plan of attack.

Separating symptoms from root causes

We know already, from Chapter 13, that these problems should be grouped and synthesized in the mind so that strategic solutions can be created. But now we must consider this key component of differentiating between the problems – we must assess which problems are manifesting purely as symptoms.

Routinely, we will be presented with any number of problems or issues during each day; however, the key challenge is learning to distinguish those that are not an issue in themselves but only a symptom of a much bigger or underlying root cause issue.

It is important to correctly identify these root causes because treating symptoms is purely palliative, and they will likely show again elsewhere or in the same place as before (or worse, a slightly different place subtly masked as something different again). This is why so many of us talk of feeling as though we are 'playing whack-a-mole', as it can seem like as soon as one thing is solved another issue pops up. These never-ending pop-ups are not always related, and in part, dealing with a great deal of pop-up issues is a trait of the role and of working with people, especially when operating at a more junior level. However, we never want to be consumed by continual pop-ups as this will quickly erode any effectiveness and risk causing derailment. This whack-a-mole feeling is a direct product of consistently attempting to treat the symptoms over the cause.

Obviously, there will be moments and circumstances where symptomatic issues or problems will have to be treated directly, without an accurate root cause identified. When an issue needs to be resolved expeditiously, it will not always be possible to say, 'Let me take that away and work up a systemic strategic-level solution to ensure this doesn't happen again'. When a person has broken their leg, our immediate response must be to treat the leg, not take steps to make sure it does not happen again – there will be time for that later. A pragmatic balance must be struck.

As discussed in Chapter 13, we should continue to mentally log and process all occurring issues as data points in the assessment of the underlying root cause problem. This process is something that we should practise every day. We should constantly be on the lookout for real life day-to-day people issues manifesting before our eyes in our business areas. The more data we have on an issue or set of issues, the more likely we are to discern the root cause of what we are seeing. This requires us to connect the dots between sometimes disparate events or occurrences. This skill is the basis of strategic ability and it is one we should begin to develop through our everyday people activities.

DOCTORS' ORDERS

When thinking about this issue of treating symptoms over root cause, it is useful to consider medical analogies so that our attention can be turned from treatment to 'diagnosis'.

In considering this analogy we should cast ourselves in the role of a medical doctor. Probably, the role of a general practitioner (GP) is the most relevant due to the vast range of initial problems and issues that can be presented before a GP on any given day. In this regard, there are similarities with the average HR business partner role for sure.

The simple analogy is this, a person presents themselves to the GP with either a single or range of symptoms, it is then the GP's role to ask investigatory questions and to conduct relevant tests, in pursuit of gaining enough insight to reach an evidence-based diagnosis. Importantly, it is only when, and if, diagnosis is reached, that a course of treatment (or in our case, a solution) can be offered.

When applied to the business world that we inhabit, this analogy hopefully demonstrates how quickly we attempt to rush to conclusions without the correct information to accurately diagnose the problem. This tends to have the unintended outcome of treating issues incorrectly because there has been no diagnosis of the root cause.

So, whilst we are always listening (Chapter 4) and continuously thinking (Chapter 13), the aim should be to use these skills to attain enough data to reach a logical and compelling diagnosis. It must be evidence based after all. Our role is to process all these human data points, through the lens of the people-expert, to produce the golden thread that all can agree is an accurate diagnosis of the problem faced.

Connecting this logical and compelling diagnosis to the frameworks developed in the previous chapter (namely, highest common factor, limitless creativity and divergence), will enable the creation of dynamic solutions that will treat the root cause, thereby eradicating the perpetually arising symptoms in one fell swoop.

Just ask why

So how do we make this assessment and determine between symptoms and root causes to reach a correct diagnosis? I have found that the most simple and effective tool in achieving this aim is to be committed to asking one question repeatedly until there are no more or deeper answers to give, and that question is a single word – *why*?

As natural problem solvers we tend to ask ourselves, 'How can we fix this?', when instead our first question should be, 'Why is this happening?' If we truly understand why an issue is occurring, then we will have a much better chance of creating strategic solutions that address the real issue.

There are a great number of ways we can potentially identify root cause issues. For the purposes of our principled approach to not treating symptoms, there is already a well-established technique we can use. I have found this technique to be useful in practice but also useful in helping us to adjust our mindset to embrace the question of 'Why is this happening?' It is the 'Five Whys technique', which was originally developed by Sakichi Toyoda, the Japanese inventor, for the Toyota Industries Corporation. The extract below succinctly describes the Five Whys technique:

> When looking to solve a problem, it helps to begin at the end result, reflect on what caused that, and question the answer five times. This elementary and often effective approach to problem solving promotes deep thinking through questioning, and can be adapted quickly and applied to most problems. Most obviously and directly, the Five Whys technique relates to the principle of systematic problem-solving: without the intent of the principle, the technique can only be a shell of the process. Hence, there are three key elements to effective use of the Five Whys technique: (i) accurate and complete statements of problems, (ii) complete honesty in answering the questions, (iii) the determination to get to the bottom of problems and resolve them. (Serrat, 2009)

Hopefully, this concept is familiar to us in some way, at least if we do not know of it directly then it will be recognizable as a technique being used by others. This description of the technique fits perfectly with our aim of seeking to identify root cause issues. Conjuring up thoughts of a parrot repeating the same phrase over and over again will be a useful mental image when pursuing this repetitive 'why' routine.

This rather blunt strategy of relentlessly deploying 'why' is necessary, because we will often find in the business of people that others have seldom done the thinking required to assess what the underlying root cause diagnosis could be. In the workplace, too many people suffer from the symptoms of something they are unable to accurately diagnose. Principally, this occurs because we are unaware of *how* to accurately diagnose these problems, and as mentioned previously, due to lack of time. It seems people would rather wrestle with what they know than risk solving something unfamiliar. I guess this is a classic case of better the devil you know, though I have always been perplexed by people who are prepared to proverbially walk with a limp when their condition is surely curable.

These trends mean that when we ask 'why' for the first time, it is very unlikely that the first answer received will be an articulate diagnosis of the root cause. In fact, it is likely that the question will need to be framed in a multitude of different manners, and from different angles of attack, to receive *any* useful or informative information as to root cause. The Five Whys technique teaches us this. If there were a killer question we could always ask to instantly determine the root cause the practice would be called the 'one why' instead!

Practising this persistent line of 'why' enquiry will enable us to produce a more accurate assessment of the real truth. A small but important warning here about 'truth' – anyone who has sat through multiple instances involving conflict between two people will know that discovering 'truth', after the fact and where people are concerned, is a virtually impossible task. As mentioned in Chapter 13, the truth required here should be sensible, logical and coherent, also it should be easily recognized by others without too much detailed explanation. I would dissuade anyone from embarking on a quest for absolute truth.

Asking 'why' will cause both the enquirer and the receiver to dig deeper into the underlying systemic factors that are impacting the existence of the symptoms they are suffering from. Much like the analogy of the iceberg, the real issue is buried deep below the surface, just because we deal with what appears to be above the water line does not mean that the whole iceberg is dealt with. What is under the surface is much more likely to cause harm and sink the ship.

A commitment to ask 'why' and pursue this course by responding to the answer given with a further inquiring 'why?', is tantamount to the doctor's investigatory questioning and relevant tests in determining the root cause of an issue. Again, we will need to embed this as a way of thinking. In every encounter with people, we should be asking ourselves the why question.

We should not rest or settle for anything less than a correct diagnosis. This correct diagnosis should be evidence based, coherent and recognizable to the people operating within the business.

Finding a cure

This concept of refusing to continually treat reoccurring symptoms, and instead insisting on identifying root cause issues, naturally leads to either treating the root or finding an eradicating cure. This is where we will need to be sure that we have shaken off our old ways. We are no longer only policy interpreters or skilled advisors. We are now strategic service designers. We must resist the urge to fix the problems (symptoms) in front of us and instead elevate our thinking to seek out a total cure. The solution-focused person will naturally be able to identify a strategic cure if there is a practical one available. If the opportunity presents itself, we must think of cure over treatment.

Returning to an idea from Chapter 13, if we have a natural interest in people this will translate into a desire to improve the working lives of others, and not to see people hamstrung by issues that affect their productivity and general well-being. If this natural interest is present in us, there will also be an ambition towards finding a lasting cure to problematic issues. We will want to cure these ills for the people we serve. In this way we discover that these too are actions which begin with a mindset – a natural interest in people, and a desire to make improvements and find a cure.

Treating symptoms is to be avoided where possible, creating an accurate diagnosis is the aim, developing strategies that treat the root causes will create impactful and lasting change, and curing the ills of the workplace is sure to cement the HR business partner in the hearts of many.

Summary

In summary, when operating at the strategic level, our focus must be on addressing root cause issues. We can easily trip ourselves up by attempting to solve the wrong issue. Our modern busyness can cause us to rush to oversimplify problems, break them down into digestible chunks and as a result create inadequate strategic solutions. Instead we should take the time to step back from individual events to think about a strategic solution that would ultimately fix them *all*. The key challenge for us is to identify issues that are not an issue in themselves but only a symptom of an underlying root cause issue. Treating symptoms is purely palliative. We must identify these root cause issues so that we can create an accurate diagnosis on which all can agree. To achieve this, we have to be relentless in asking 'why?' and pursuing the answer to why a thing is occurring. Pursuit of why will enable everyone to dig deeper into the systemic issues affecting the business and its people. Once a diagnosis is made, we will be free to pursue a cure, throwing off treatments in favour of a total eradication of the issues.

Next, we will explore the final chapter of 'The clever stuff' – the ever-important art of storytelling.

Reference

Serrat, O (2009) *The Five Whys Technique*, Asian Development Bank, February [online] https://www.adb.org/sites/default/files/publication/27641/five-whys-technique.pdf (archived at https://perma.cc/DA65-ZHME)

15

Tell me a story

When facts are not enough

This is still the clever stuff, so we could not round out Part Four without considering the benefits of developing the skill of storytelling. This ability is intertwined with the strategic mindset and as with Chapter 14, 'Don't treat the symptoms', is a further essential branch that needs to be grown from the strategic mindset tree.

Much like our foundational structure, the clever stuff is also tripartite in nature. With our foundational structure there is an order: we must first know HR, then the business, after which we can add value. These are equal parts that will counterbalance each other, provided they are learned and applied in the correct order. There is also an order with the clever stuff but only in so much as the strategic mindset must come first. What is added to the strategic mindset can be added in any order. So, with the clever stuff, the parts are less equal. Instead it is the strategic mind that is primary and central, and the focus on root causes and now storytelling that hang from this central mindset pillar, are secondary.

Over the length of our existence, HR business partners, and HR professionals in general, have progressively embraced the use of data to drive insights and decision making. The use of data to inform people-related matters is an important and essential part of the HR and business partnering offering. Presenting data in a way that business leaders can then use to draw conclusions and drive action is a skill in itself. Fortunately, this is a discipline that many of us have become versed in and an area which HR functions are developing all the time. As a result, many of us are now comfortable with taking an evidence-based approach to our work.

However, there still exists a sometimes-wide corridor between the answers provided by the data and a group of leaders, or 'cavepeople', taking the hard decision to follow the right course of action. Sometimes the data is just not enough on its own to convince the required people to approve a direction or solution.

The data does not know the minds of the decision makers. Data does not intimately know and understand the power dynamics within the room. Data does not know the environmental factors that impact the decision-making process. When the facts on their own are not sufficient to influence the right outcome, a human intervention is needed. A people-expert is required to step into this gap and manually synthesize these factors that will ultimately influence the decision-making process. This is where the business's people-expert needs to step in to bridge the gap between the data and the decision.

This is the moment where we need to go beyond the data, beyond the evidence, to weave together a true and compelling narrative that can capture the hearts and minds of the listeners to drive effective decision making. We can do this because we know HR, know the business and have a propensity for adding value. Furthermore, our understanding of the people fundamentals enables us to listen and empathize effectively whilst maintaining the humility to not over impose our own views in place of those we serve.

The data of course is used to underpin the story, but it is the composition and telling of the story that does the required influencing. Where the facts end, the story must begin.

The margin of misunderstanding

Whilst we do not need to operate the clever stuff in an order, aside from placing the strategic mindset first, there is a definite benefit to telling compelling stories about issues where we have *already* defined the root cause(s). If we are seeking to resolve a problem through the lens of storytelling to influence an outcome, then we had better be certain about the root causes first. In all other circumstances where storytelling is useful, we may not need to have deployed the deep analysis required to identify root cause issues. Sometimes, storytelling is simply a great medium to engage with others and help people to understand otherwise difficult or complex problems more easily.

However, if we embed a strategic mindset and then seek out root cause issues, we will then need to turn our attention to *how* we explain our trail of thought to others. This is where our strategic mindset comes to life. At this moment the root cause problem and corresponding creative solution ceases to exist only in our minds when we share it with a relevant person who is familiar with the matter. The problem with sharing the inner workings of your own brain with others is that they do not think like you do and they certainly do not share your brain. Sometimes, this can affect the extent to which we are understood by others. Simply and succinctly communicating the discovery of the root cause of a complex problem can be a long and confusing process. A lot can be lost in translation. It is easy to understand things that we have formulated in our own minds, but much harder to communicate them to others so that they share our understanding. If there is a lack of understanding, then there is a risk that the problem and hard-forged solution will fall on deaf ears.

Having done the serious work of listening, analysing, asking why, thinking deeply and creating viable solutions, it would be a terrible shame to fall at the final hurdle when communicating to others how and why this approach will be successful.

Part of the problem of course, is that we must explain this thought process and conceptualized solution to another *person*. These other people will have their own experiences, preferences, biases and preconceived ideas through which they will process our proposed solutions. We experience this every time someone responds to our well-formed suggestions with, 'We tried that before, it didn't work'. Inputting this data into a machine would be far easier!

For HR business partners trying to convince business leaders to our viewpoint on matters concerning their business, the problem deepens because leaders already have their own thoughts and feelings on the subject at hand. These pre-existing conditions of mind must be considered when trying to convince leaders of a proposed root cause treatment. When you add in that these problems are always related to people, we often encounter the additional leadership condition of, 'I'm human, so that makes me a people-expert'. This condition has come up already on our journey so I will not go into the depths of detail on this point. Suffice to say, when this condition is exhibited in the most senior of business leaders it can be particularly problematic and negatively impact the people within their sphere of leadership.

In leadership and in HR business partnering, we should all be slow to speak and quick to listen. If any of us have systemic failings in this area it is likely that the margin for misunderstanding will widen. Whether these failings exist in ourselves or in others, we should be aware of this when considering how we lead, how we influence, how we engage, how we communicate and how we tell stories.

Our role exists in the grey of people matters to ensure that this margin for misunderstanding is reduced or removed altogether. To achieve this, we need to be able to build and tell compelling narratives that illustrate the case for change. Being heard above the noise and finding allies in this endeavour can be difficult tasks. We can only use these tools and hope that if we have proven to be the true people-expert that others will begin to listen.

The strategic influencer instruments

Routinely, we tell HR business partners that they 'must be a great influencer'. This advice comes from all angles both inside and outside of the HR function. Infrequently does the advice on *how* to universally achieve this difficult feat extend much beyond this statement. At the risk of repeating myself, this trend towards us being offered multiple 'whats' to the exclusion of *any* 'hows', is my main motivation in writing for the HR business partner community. I believe this strategic influencer requirement is another of those areas where we are flush with the 'what' but deficient in the 'how'. Most of us already know what to do, it is the how that we need help with.

One of the strategic influencing 'hows' available to us is the ability to create new ideas and solutions. This is the limitless creativity 'instrument' that we have at our disposal as already discussed in Chapter 13. However, in matters of influence, it is not enough to rely on the unfiltered ideas themselves to do the convincing and conversion. Thinking about other common ways we can influence others, it is also not enough to rely solely on articulate speech, trusted relationships and charisma to win the hearts and minds of all involved. Although these things should get us through the door and, at the very least, given a good hearing. These great ideas will need some careful packaging before they can be presented.

Having harnessed the strategic mindset, discovered the root causes, and created compelling problem statements with corresponding effective solutions, the final part of 'The clever stuff' is to sum it all up in a powerful and ingenious tale that creates the forward case for change. In this difficult task of communicating and convincing people of strategic concepts and corresponding strategic-level solutions, we had better be equipped with an even greater tool to achieve our proselytizing – that tool is the story.

In the last two chapters we have already talked about problem statements and corresponding solutions needing to be both compelling and coherent in the relevant circumstances. At this point in the outworking of the strategic mindset, people need to be convinced, not just of an accurate problem statement, but of a workable-seen-to-be-potentially-successful proposed solution. This means that what is offered must be presented in a compelling way so as to come to life in the context of the real world. These strategic thoughts and ideas become far easier to grasp if they are more than just conceptual musings. The consideration of real-world application sorts the wheat from the chaff. This is the practical 'instrument' that we unpacked in Chapter 12.

Hypothetical scenarios and conceptualizations can also be useful tools. They are the embryos of this art of storytelling that we are exploring. However, conceptualizing and mapping scenarios as tools is useful when trying to assess the full range of potential options, but may not go far enough when we are attempting to convince people of a final definite direction of travel. Getting agreement will require a solution to be both creative and practical.

When moving through this narrow zone of bringing all hearts and minds to agreement on a single direction of travel, it is important to harness the potency of belief. Vivid proselytization (conversion to a belief) is the fuel that drives the hearts and minds of people. In the world of business, it is easy to overlook the matter of belief, but we should always remember to connect the dots to build solutions that people will believe in. Who knew that the HR business partner was also required to be an evangelist!

To forge a new or difficult path people need to be shown something, or someone, to believe in. When it comes to the local business areas people, we have a significant and fundamental role to play in the creation of the 'something' to believe in. Business leaders should look to lead their people in this way through the creation of shared belief in our work. It is HR business partners, as the resident business area people-expert, who should use their people and business knowledge to influence how these beliefs are constructed.

This is where the effectiveness of storytelling and the power of the narrative really comes to the fore. This fact prevails: all people, including our 'cavepeople', connect best with our stories as opposed to generic concepts or unproven ideas.

On this point of things to believe in, clearly it is also our role to contribute to the creation of a person that people want to follow – the 'someone' to believe in. We should be wary to ensure we are not becoming that person ourselves – although if our presence is reassuring to the people then that will help greatly. We have not covered this directly in detail, but it is self-evident that if we are a people-expert then we should have the effect of making the leaders we serve better at leading their people. People-experts by default will be effective encouragers and coaches who naturally enable senior leaders to become better leaders of people. This is a standard by-product of effective and successful HR business partnering – the presence of a decent and competent HR business partner should improve the people leadership abilities of others around them. Hopefully this is a recognizable HR business partner trait.

When telling our stories, we will need to leverage our strategic influencer instruments of creativity, practicality and belief. This means our stories must be novel, applicable to the real world in which we operate, and compelling to draw others to them.

A story with a purpose

These stories we weave have a number of key uses and benefits. We have already touched upon how a story can connect with people on the belief level, meaning they are more likely to be converted to an idea if they believe in it. If people believe the story to represent a truth then it is far more likely to 'stick' and become part of the future patchwork of the organization's, or individual business area's, culture. We will know we have been truly successful if a story we have directed becomes retold to the point of becoming a part of the culture. However, organizational cultures can be made up of many different stories, positive and negative, historical and current. As most of us will already know, organizational development practitioners commonly describe this phenomenon as 'stories and myths' (Kaye, 1995). In practice, these stories are passed on between colleagues over time, as if handed down from generation to generation within a family line. This process then often skews the original facts over time and the true reality of a circumstance can easily be lost or forgotten. For these reasons we should be careful that we construct our narratives, so they are simply retold and quick to correct inaccurate explanations.

One of the functional benefits of using stories to explain strategic thoughts and ideas is that the story makes the strategy easier to explain. A good strategy is a simple strategy. For the people-expert, simplicity in people strategies is desirable but there are inevitably many nuances at play when we start thinking up strategic approaches to our people problems. This is where the story comes into play, bringing to life that which *can* be difficult to explain simply. The shoehorning of deeply nuanced people ideas into an eloquent story will circumnavigate misunderstanding in the hearing.

Another key advantage of presenting strategic thought in story form is that it is far easier to recall, and therefore, more importantly, far easier to retell to others. For a story to be successful it must be retold by someone other than the originator. Stories can spread far quicker, and understanding be embedded more effectively, than that which could be achieved with any corporate strategy diagram. Especially one that has been designed by an external agency at great cost and time commitment to the organization! There can be great value in a good clear strategy diagram, but unfortunately, they just aren't half as powerful as a compelling narrative retold continually amongst colleagues over time.

Stories breed. A good story will be retold many times over, whether to internal colleagues, new hires, customers, clients or other stakeholders. The person-to-person retelling of a story is powerful, not just in continuing to convert the person telling the story themselves, but also in the conversion of all those around them who hear and come to recognize the story each time it is retold. There is a remarkable response in people who, on hearing a repeated or recognizable story, will feel absolutely compelled to thrust themselves forward and declare that they too are already aware of the story being told and also advocate for it. When it comes to storytelling, we seem to have a strong desire to be included in the narrative. We need to associate with it and find ourselves in the story. There must be something about this scenario that triggers our natural fear of missing out, as if it would be so terrible to be the new person who did not know the full patchwork of organizational stories. It seems that in the case of storytelling, familiarity breeds a reassuring comfort, instead of the usual contempt with which we all associate familiarity.

A well-composed story can connect an abstract idea to a person's reality, and thereby cause them to begin to change and adapt their behaviour, in pursuit of bringing the story to life. This is one of the implicit implications of compelling stories retold – the retelling is always performed with an underlying purpose. That purpose usually being to encourage people to start, or just as common, to stop, behaving in a certain way. The story is often subtly deployed to induce conformality. People love nothing more than fitting in. Stories help us to connect with each other and create the required link and shared purpose we need to feel part of a team. Success can also be easily measured though the telling of stories. A coherent story that starts at 'point A' and maps a journey to 'point B' creates a simple method of assessing progress against a goal or direction of travel. This kind of assessment of progress is also a very inclusive process, no one is left out of having an opinion on 'how things are going' with this strategic direction.

A good story can be the hook people need to understand why we are all thinking and behaving in a certain way. Behaviour and language that seem strange from the outside looking in become very natural for those who are a part of the shared story. Once people hear and understand the story, they become part of the fabric, woven together with others who also know and appreciate the power of the story. In this way, it is this retelling of stories that creates new leaders and new followers, all of whom successfully achieve behaviour change through a shared vision expounded by the medium of storytelling.

This is the type of storytelling that carries real purpose.

Deliberate and directional storytelling

On a tactical level, stories can also be quickly created to prevent people from falling into an undesired way of thinking or speaking.

Often in business there will be any number of negative narratives in circulation. This is entirely normal, but negative narratives do require us to be aware of them and keep a close-watching brief for how they might develop. These negative narratives are often accompanied by certain underpinning phrases or words that the business's leaders would rather did not exist and were not used. A simple and common example of this is where the past is constantly talked about to justify decisions and actions in the present and future. Where this behaviour is acute, it is the definition of being held back by our past (which can often be a past that many of the present people were not party to).

For the most part this trait of looking back is often unhelpful, and decisions about the present and future need to be taken with reference to where we are going, not where we have already been. Targeted narrative and story can be used to replace these would-be prohibitive stories and phrases with clever pivots or delicate reframing that fundamentally change the spoken narrative. Managing these negative narratives is essential when we are seeking to galvanize people around a shared vision or story.

This is perhaps the easiest type of behaviour change – the overlaying of old and outdated stories with new and exciting visions of the future. It is remarkable the instant change that can be achieved in most people by simply getting them to look forward instead of backward. This is the seed of fundamental culture change.

In this area of storytelling, *our* challenge is to move from our traditional comfort zone of explaining processes, policies and systems, to telling engaging and compelling stories in this strategic realm. This will be a kind of step-change for anyone not versed in this discipline. Having already put on the strategic mindset, this idea of progressing into storytelling may appear a further mindset to adopt, but it is just a natural and necessary progression of the strategic mindset. So, in this way we need to use the strategic mindset to consider how we use storytelling to articulate our strategic-level thinking. Demonstration and application of this skill is a telltale sign that we have arrived at our strategic destination.

The very best stories will be absolutely rooted in fact. These types of stories will ring true to those who hear them. People will learn from the past if it can be well summarized and made accessible to both those who did and did not experience it directly.

People are already learning from their own, or others', organizational experience, so shouldn't we be intervening to deliberately guide and direct this narrative rather than being on the receiving end of whatever the loudest voice chooses to shout about?

Anyone who has experienced the long-suffering ill effects of damaging organizational storytelling will know that it can create a really helpless feeling within organizations and individual teams. These ill effects are particularly damaging when it comes to people believing in the likelihood of success when implementing change. It is all too easy for people to become stuck at the bottom of the change curve (Kübler-Ross, 1969) due to the absence of a deliberate and positive narrative. The 'nothing ever changes' brigade really can be self-fulfilling prophets.

Personally, I would rather direct the telling of positive organizational narrative than be suffering from the long-lasting effects of negative or unhelpful storytelling. People need a story to be told, and as the business's people-expert we should be the ones to tell it.

Summary

In summary, the ability of storytelling is intertwined with the strategic mindset. Sometimes an evidence-based approach is insufficient and the data fails to influence our humanity. This is where we play a vital role as the people-expert in the business. We use our knowledge and skill to bridge the gap between the data and the correct course of action. Storytelling has many uses and is a great tool to enable understanding of difficult or complex problems. There are many factors to consider when trying to convince another person of a root cause diagnosis. We will need to apply our knowledge of the business, its people and its leaders to successfully weave stories that they recognize and understand. To tell a powerful story we need to leverage our strategic influencer instruments of creativity, practicality and belief. We should approach our stories as beliefs and seek to lead people through the process of conversion. People are more likely to be converted to an idea if they believe in it. We should realize the heritage that 'stories and myths' have within our businesses. This history tells us that stories breed. A good story will be told many times over. We can harness the purpose of a good story to drive the behaviours we want to see within a business in pursuit of achieving organizational goals. There is great power in stories that connect and create the shared purpose we need to feel part of a team. Finally, our new stories can be used to dispel negative narratives or unhelpful past stories that hold us back from future progress. These are the tactical stories told just in the nick of time to bring hope of a brighter future and light to the end of the dark tunnel.

This brings us to the end of Part Four, 'The clever stuff'. Only these three chapters were required because, as I have already said, becoming strategic is nine-tenths preparatory. Next, we must turn our attention to ensuring our and others' longevity and sustainability on this journey. In Part Five we will close with 'The warning signs'.

References

Kaye, M (1995) Organisational myths and storytelling as communication management: a conceptual framework for learning an organisation's culture, *Journal of Management & Organization*, **1** (2), pp 1–13

Kübler-Ross, E (1969) *On Death and Dying*, Macmillan Publishing Co

The warning signs

The world of HR can be a difficult place to navigate successfully. Something about blending the realms of people and business, trying to exist within this and then bridge the gap between the two, can lead to some considerable pain.

Many of us have been burnt in different ways down the years. Some of us bear the scars and others have burnt out completely.

Whilst not wishing to finish on a downer, it seems only right and prudent that I not mislead those with less experience and instead call out some of the most prevalent and problematic issues experienced by diligent and long-serving HR business partners.

It was not my intention to leave these things until last, but having moved from foundations to fundamentals, through to strategic, it seems to me that this is where these warning signs most commonly occur in the story. Something about success and longevity tends to create a breeding ground for the issues I will lay out in this section.

Of course, the best way to navigate these issues is to experience them for yourself and learn from them. However, as I have already pointed out, it is the wisest of people who can successfully learn from the mistakes of others therefore negating the need to exclusively learn from their own mistakes. I am aiming here to give some people that opportunity to be included in with the wisest.

I hope to be able to herald some warnings to shine a light for those who may not yet have seen these signs. And for those who are in the midst of these issues, I hope my words can act for some as a cease and desist order and for others a route out of a difficult or confusing juncture.

Knowing the sound of these warning signs will hopefully be enough to steer the hearer clear of the rocks that can cause terminal damage.

16

Don't throw nuts

The Destiny of Man is to unite, not to divide. If you keep on dividing, you end up as a collection of monkeys throwing nuts at each other out of separate trees.

T H WHITE (1958)

Separate trees

Before we begin with this subject, and this section, I must remind us that we are now discussing the 'warning signs'. These are some of the key and prevalent conditions that can limit us or cause us to stumble. Hopefully these are conditions that you have yet to experience therefore providing you with a reasonable chance to heed the warning.

Our first warning sign is essentially concerned with the condition of infighting. This kind of concealed conflict or competitiveness has negative effects on teams of HR business partners and HR functions.

Before we dive into the depths of this awkward subject, I am mindful of those who may never have experienced this infighting condition, so I first want to address the circumstances where it is less likely to exist. I specify these circumstances in the hope that they do indeed prevent this condition from being universal everywhere there are teams of HR business partners.

I believe there are perhaps two circumstances where this unfortunate condition does not prevail. Firstly, this is less likely to happen, or to be problematic, in smaller organizations where there are perhaps only two or three HR business partner roles. The tendency for shared experiences in these smaller settings (or in this case, shared enemies!) helps us to band together in the performance of our roles. This is a structural mitigator that often means infighting is less prevalent. However, the size of an organization is outside the control of HR business partners and therefore this factor is only incidental in treating the condition. And of course, there is no absolute mitigation for discovering that two colleagues simply do not get on with each other.

So secondly, and more significantly, concealed conflict and negative competitiveness is less likely to occur where there is a tendency for consistency within the HR business partnering function. By consistency I simply mean a drive towards offering the same services, in a similar way, at the same time. Consistency in this context also means providing the same answers to the same or similar questions. This consistency approach allows less room for individual deviation (and also, less room for individual personality).

This consistency is normally achieved by teams meeting regularly or regularly sharing their latest updates, problems and queries with the group. It seems that to achieve a greater level of consistency requires us to share more of our general day-to-day decision making with each other. Perhaps it is this exposing process that helps to build deeper levels of transparency and trust, thereby negating the problematic competitive infighting condition. This consistency limits the power of individual HR business partners to deviate too often or too far from the party line. This all seems to have the effect of creating a more consistent, aligned and tighter-knit HR business partnering team but at the expense of the close business alignment that many of us are known for.

Please note that I am not necessarily advocating for this type of consistency as a rule for teams of HR business partners. I am purely pointing out that I believe this trend towards consistency means that there will be no separate trees from which to throw nuts.

Division

Now that we have established the circumstances that are less likely to create division between teams, we can turn our attention to the attributes of the problem itself where we find that it persists.

HR business partners can be strange creatures. It seems that in every medium to large size organization there is a reasonable chance of finding an atypical person who breaks the mould of HR business partnering as we thought we knew it, but unfortunately, not in a positive way.

There exists a certain type of HR business partner who through their own actions, makes their own lives, and the lives of others, far more difficult than they need be. They may appear unnecessarily combative within the business partner team or behave as if every interaction between peers is in fact a competition with winners and losers. Others will find themselves being careful what they say around them, realizing that honesty is perceived as weakness and quickly punished. At times these individuals will seem to disagree simply for the sake of it and go out of their way to find fault with what others say or do. The mistakes of others are pounced upon and held aloft so they and others know all the gory details. Their subordinates are often unable to move for fear of making the wrong decision and top cover, in the form of a more senior leader, never seems to come to their rescue. They seem to have a never-ending supply of buses under which to throw people.

Their approach seems to be reliant upon taking control within a team of equal peers by setting out to covertly or overtly pick apart others' characters and their work. Individual recipients of this approach are mostly unmerited of it, and the purpose seems to be to push others down so that one can be seen to be elevated amongst the crowd. As if other HR business partner peers represent some kind of existential threat. I do not believe this practice could be condoned even if it were proven in certain circumstances to hold any merit. This type of behaviour cannot be a good or appropriate example of the means justifying the end.

One person acting in this way within a team has the effect of creating a deep and widespread dysfunction at both the individual and team levels. It is a behaviour that relies on divisiveness for success. Such is the disruption that it puts other members of the team on the spot and requires them to pick a side, or at the very least to entertain the ideas of an individual's dogma. This penchant for divisiveness naturally creates cracks within team loyalties and relationships.

Unfortunately, these behaviours are more than an individual just 'not being a team player', it tends to run deeper than that.

Inexorable insecurities

This type of behaviour by one person within a team would, you hope, usually be quickly shut down by others or by the relevant manager. However, the perpetrator's behaviour and actions can be quite veiled or indirect, allowing them to operate below the radar of serious repercussions. The common denominator with these atypical individuals who exhibit this behaviour is that they seem to be able to perform to just the right level to keep themselves out of any serious trouble. Or, they have some important specific knowledge or specialism that demonstrates their obvious value to the team. They are perceived as competent and value adding and thereby manage to avoid any detailed scrutiny.

Scrutiny of their own houses also tends to be overlooked, because the essence of this strategy is to deflect attention away from themselves and instead cast the cloud of doubt over others. As a result, people do not immediately notice the flaws in the accuser, especially as they are consumed by looking elsewhere. Or, we are apparently prepared to look past potential flaws in the accuser to instead investigate the apparent accusations raised about others. The unfortunate tactic here is to reduce the belief in another's strengths to cause division amongst the team.

At times we look kindly upon these accusers or we pass this behaviour off as being 'just the way that they are', but when examined closely it is difficult not to admit that there is a clever type of manipulation in operation. My own assessment of this kind of manipulative approach is that it is rooted in some kind of inexorable insecurity.

I believe that it is best to live our lives in a way that we see, or at least look for, the best in people. Therefore, I find it difficult to conclude that anyone would intentionally *choose* this approach as the best course of action. I have known self-confessed narcissists and borderline clinical psychopaths, but neither of these conditions align neatly with the atypical individuals I am describing here.

Instead, I think these behaviours manifested are the product of a simple, but toxic, combination of insecurity and fear. It is a kind of lucidity of mind and an acute awareness of one's own shortcomings, which creates a set of irrational fears. These irrational fears in turn cause a person to lash out at, or oppress, others who through their own entirely adequate performance could prove a threat by exposing these holes.

One of the most interesting features of this type of atypical individual is their wide-ranging polymorphic abilities. They will appear to take on various forms at different times and, mostly, do this in the company of different groups of people. This is most likely to be recognizable as two-faced behaviour. For individuals exhibiting these behaviours, it will seem no problem to support an approach in one room and simultaneously speak out against it in another. On a more subtle level, the taking on of different forms will be used to encourage others to trust them when there is really no serious intention of behaving in a trustworthy manner.

The general proclivity for adaptability is usually a trait for us to hold in high regard; however, *here* it is misappropriated and twisted to entirely serve the needs of an individual as opposed to a business function or an organizational purpose. Changeability purely for one's own personal gain is often disingenuous and deceitful. Whilst it does take time to discern these sometimes subtle behaviours, it is likely that this adaptability in atypical individuals is another form of active manipulation at work.

Ultimately, HR business partners who exhibit these behaviours and operate in this way, whilst having some success in undertaking their business area activity, will inevitably cause division with their colleagues, within their teams and ultimately the HR function at large. This division will quickly be noticed by the business too. The most perceptive of people external to the HR function will realize that not all is well in HR land. Whilst loyalties usually run deep between HR business partners and business area leaders, this realization usually gives managers a degree of discomfort about their own HR business partner, even if they are performing well for the individual business area. This is not a desirable position for anyone to find themselves in.

I find that this disruption is, for the most part, entirely unnecessary and unwarranted. In general terms, I am an advocate for disruption. I believe the status quo should be challenged, we should ask 'why', and we should seek out positive change. *This* type of disruption is borne out of a natural interest in people. The key attribute of this type of disruption is that it is rooted in improving the lives of others. Conversely, I am yet to observe a truly decent and morally righteous use for the type of destructive disruption that I am warning against here.

There must be a better way. One bad apple should not be allowed to spoil the whole barrel.

Separation anxiety

To delve deeper into the causal factors of infighting we need to consider the structural effects that can play a key role. At the beginning of this chapter we explored consistency as a means by which much of this condition is mitigated. Here we must then consider the opposite of consistency and its effects.

By nature, HR business partnering teams are made up of a collection of individuals who, generally, serve separate and discrete business areas. This structure of servicing discreet business areas creates degrees of separation, meaning that for most delivery activity, we operate completely separately from each other.

Moreover, the historical trend toward being physically co-located within business areas has meant a further separation for teams of HR business partners. This common practice means that many individuals only come together with other HR peers, and the wider HR function, for monthly or quarterly team meetings. The policy of physical co-location was never intended to be about separation from HR colleagues but always about 'being closer to the business'. However, separation from HR is the unintended consequence.

This separation can be good for the individual business areas. This is because they often get a dedicated resource they can see and call upon at all times without the day-to-day 'distractions' of the pull of the wider HR function. We have already explored the requirements for us to 'know the business' in Chapter 2, and a little separation from the HR function to pursue this aim is required. However, too much separation is not necessarily good for the HR function or for teams of HR business partners. The larger and more geo-diverse the team the more acute the problem – people can easily go weeks without interacting with each other.

This separation creates a lack of camaraderie and at times a lack of common and shared goals. The separation is exacerbated further if two individuals are serving different business areas that themselves are at odds or in conflict with each other. In these circumstances, the prerequisite separation tends to lead people to pledge allegiance to their respective business areas, and not the HR function or the HR business partner team. The unfortunate product of this scenario can be the pitting of HR business partners against one another. This scenario creates disagreement between HR business partners who are both backing the respective views of their different business areas. What works for one will not necessarily work for all. This can then lead to problematic issues of consistency or precedent in the application of organizational policy.

This paradigm does not help to create healthy and mutually encouraging teams of HR business partners; instead it can mean that HR colleagues decline to share key decisions that may impact upon others in future. However, I do not believe it is the sole source of the issue of atypical nut-throwing individuals.

Comfortable with conflict

As HR generalists with backgrounds rooted in advisory, another of our natural features probably contributes to this propensity for nut throwing. We must, to some extent, be comfortable with conflict.

Many of us have been preconditioned to conflict having grown up in the HR profession. We have been required to be central figures in conflict management as well as undertaking grievance, sickness and disciplinary meetings in difficult circumstances, sometimes dealing with people who are having extreme emotional reactions to the processes we are administering. There are times where we have had to dismiss people because it is the right thing to do, even though we can see the impact it will have on them and their families. This is a hard role for anyone, especially for those with a genuine interest in people.

Perhaps this thick skin, developed out of necessity, creates a new and naturally higher threshold for everyday conflict with others. Perhaps the threshold for conflict is built in the same way we build muscle in the body – the greater the weight, the greater the gain. Maybe these higher thresholds for conflict are a contributary factor in the elevated levels of unpleasantness that can at times exist across cadres of HR business partners.

Overall, though, I expect that the most significant factors triggering this condition will be a person's own state of being informed by their personal traits, past experiences and self-perception – those inexorable insecurities. It is a problem distinctly individual in the making, even if some environmental and structural factors have a contributory impact. Before we get too carried away with the problems of HR business partners, I rather suspect that this problem and condition are well-recognized in the business world far beyond only the HR profession.

Our partners in promotion

I have found that it is difficult to change who people think themselves to be and therefore, in writing this book, I expect to have little success here in changing the personas of these nut throwers. Rather than attempting to dissuade people from a pre-existing course of action, I instead want to provide an alternative and urge us to look to what we *should* all be doing in the encouragement and building up of each other within the profession.

As strange as this may sound, in 2015 I began to explore my passion for music and exercise my lifelong ambition of starting a record label. In preparation for this foray into another discipline and industry I completed a music business diploma. It was during this course that the tutor corrected my error in understanding who would be my competitors within the music industry. He explained to me that other record labels were not my competitors because they were the people who were also sharing the burden of championing the promotion of my same genre of music (Melhuish, 2015). The presence of other players within the same genre and industry enhanced my chances of success, not decreased them. Some years on this still seems to be a profound point. Those that you naturally assume to be your competition are in fact your partners in promotion, to the mutual benefit and prosperity of all involved.

The same can be true of us as individual HR business partners. There are occasions where we can be led to look across the table at each other with slightly suspicious vision, carefully watching each other's every move for the slightest indication of underhandedness or wrongdoing. You may encounter situations where being in competition with each other seems to have become embedded in our psyche. Too often we come to see each other as competitors rather than collaborators or joint-venture partners. Just like the record label analogy, we have an error in our understanding. Somehow the system, or the people contributing to the operation of the system, has failed us, or at the very least, has a propensity to lead us astray. It is essential that we all correct this error in our understanding. Many of the negative things that are spoken of us have their root cause in this error of understanding. For others looking in on a set of over-competitive and in-fighting HR business partners, it does nothing for the perception of the role, its function or the HR function overall.

The solution to this problem is recognizing that we are not in competition with each other. We have spent so much time building trust and credibility within our business areas that it seems illogical not to expend our energy in building the same level of trust with our HR business partner colleagues, and the HR function more widely. Again, this trust is more readily achieved where there is a trend for consistency and collaboration, as opposed to separation and division. Understanding that we are all jointly sharing the burden of championing the organization's aims and objectives is the first step towards building this mutual trust.

This may be a slightly simplified point, but sometimes if we could fix the conflict amongst our own ranks, we would have a far better shot at achieving organizational consistency and harmony.

Crab mentality

What we should instead be doing is encouraging each other and pulling others up, not pushing each other down. Just like crabs in a bucket we can be prone to pulling each other down or holding each other back. Learning instead to propel each other forward is what we need to be doing to drive our profession into the future. Part of this is also using our innate abilities to spot and nurture potential future talent who are further back on the journey and give them the support they need to succeed.

There is a vast amount of knowledge and capability within our teams, which means there is a lot that can be learnt from each other. A propensity for encouraging and equipping each other in all areas of our work will go a long way toward expediting the success of HR business partnering as a whole. I am not only talking at an organizational level; I mean at a worldwide industry-of-people profession level. Who knows, with the right approach, maybe, just maybe, we could even band together to change the world!

A lot of time has passed since the introduction of the HR business partner concept in the 1990s, after having taken many years to master the big strategic question, could it just be our own selves that are holding back the profession from its rightful place at the heart of all people-driven business? Is our future success as simple as eliminating the in-fighting and intra-organizational competition in order to reach the Ulrich-prophesied utopia? Perhaps. I would of course advocate for at least giving it a try in pursuit of discovering the truth.

I think the ultimate solution to all of this is to be intentionally committed to a conscious honesty of thought, being prepared to throw off the leading of our own emotions and instead operate by the application of an honest mind. This is a simple equation, firstly requiring us to be honest with ourselves, and secondly to be honest with those around us. Simple to explain but much harder to achieve.

This issue requires people to change their own hearts and minds. This will be a difficult task for sure. As you likely will know already from first-hand experience, changing the hearts and minds of others is a tricky and often fruitless business. This is something we will need to do for ourselves. An honest self-assessment will be required. We must face these difficult truths where they exist and decide for ourselves what we will each do in pursuit of improvement. Only then can we hope that these hard truths will set us free.

Summary

In summary, this condition of infighting can be more likely to occur where the requirement for consistency amongst HR business partners is lacking. This consistency approach allows less room for individual deviation and therefore fewer moments for conflict to arise amongst colleagues. In medium to large organizations there is a chance of finding an atypical HR business partner who is unnecessarily combative, and who makes life more difficult for their other HR colleagues. This is a divisive behaviour that can create deep dysfunction. Individuals who exhibit this behaviour tend to go unpunished. Others tend to give them a wide berth or normalize the behaviour by saying 'that's just the way they are'. These atypical individuals' actions are often driven by a combination of insecurity and fear. This toxic combination causes a person to lash out at their colleagues who they believe could pose a threat just by being competent. If consistency mitigates infighting, then physical separation can exacerbate this condition. Working separately on discrete business areas and having reduced interaction is not conducive to reducing the instances of differences and infighting. Physical separation can lead to a lack of camaraderie and at times a lack of shared goals. Given the nature of our roles and our likely career paths, many of us have long since been comfortable with conflict. Perhaps this thick skin, developed out of necessity, creates a new and naturally higher threshold for everyday conflict with others. Seeking a solution to this problem, we should embrace the idea that we are not in competition with other HR business partners. It is essential that we all correct this error in our understanding. Instead, we are all partners in the promotion of the HR business partnering function and the wider services and offerings of the HR function. Therefore, we should be encouraging each other and pulling each other up. We should always avoid behaving like crabs in a bucket.

Next, we will explore another of our warning signs – the tricky subject of promotion.

References

Melhuish, S (2015) Music Business School [online] https://www.musicbusinessschool.co.uk/ (archived at https://perma.cc/SWP6-49LD)

White, T H (1958) *The Once and Future King*, Collins, London

17

Progression over promotion

Our ultimate destination

Throughout this book I have referred, either directly or indirectly, to the assumption that we will mostly likely have started our HR career in a junior position and have been promoted up through the advisory ranks to an HR business partner type role. This assumption is, of course, based on my own experience, but also what I have long observed to be a general trend in the progression from administrator/coordinator to advisory to business partnering roles.

Now we must deal with what comes *after* this successive stream of successful promotions. Where do we go once we have arrived at our ultimate destination of attaining the sought-after title and becoming a bona fide HR business partner? What is to be done when the ceiling is reached?

Perhaps some of us already had ingrained aspirations far beyond the role of HR business partner and the opportunity was not a destination but instead a stepping stone to something even bigger; a means, not an end. As a result, many former HR business partners have long-since progressed onto leading HR functions and tackling director-level challenges. However, for every person who has been promoted beyond the role it feels as though there are at least five who have not. Even that is perhaps generous, it is probably more like 10 or more who have not been promoted beyond the role for every person who has been.

Maybe this admission will prove to be a little embarrassing, but for me, once I had a small taste of what the people profession had to offer, my only goal was to become a fully fledged card-carrying HR business partner. I did not automatically look much beyond that. Given I was very junior at the time this aim would have been fairly aspirational. It would take me several steps (and many years) to achieve this goal, and in fact there was no guarantee that I would be able to achieve it at all. This was an ambitious plan, a decent stretch target, but it was by no means a complete career plan. For me personally, I had really given no thought to what I might want to do once I had achieved this lofty lifetime aim of becoming an HR business partner.

I think many other well-meaning individuals can also suffer from this condition of ambitious but ultimately limited aspirations. We see ahead to the future but perhaps not far enough or not quite the whole picture. It is easiest to aspire to what is just ahead of us, or perhaps a few steps further on. However, it is much harder for us to plan out whole careers and to know what we might want at different points in our careers before we reach those points. This trait is surprisingly common amongst many, including beyond the HR function. All too often when asked about career aspirations we struggle to trot out anything other than the next role up in their current line-management structure.

In my own personal journey, however, once I had reached my goal of becoming an HR business partner, attaining this level and enjoying some success in the role, it seemed to become more natural to think that I could progress onto a head of HR or HR director role. I am not sure if this thought was entirely of my own doing or if it was placed there by others, or a little of both. This was never my original intention, but it slowly crept into my thinking somehow. Having these ambitions in itself is of course no bad thing but they do need to be tested and weighed and our motivation checked before we head off down a path without proper consideration. It seems that we are now pre-programmed to always be on the lookout for the next new opportunity, as if what we already have is enough for today but entirely unsatisfactory for tomorrow.

Any successful and celebrated individual must wrestle with this challenge – why is it not enough to *only* be a great HR business partner, why does one feel the pressure to have to move on up?

A VOCATIONAL CHALLENGE

This question of promotion is common to most disciplines, but I find it to be most acute in our roles because, as I have shared already, in my view HR business partnering is something of a vocation.

You can accuse me of being melodramatic, but I think there are many of us who can see the roles we play on behalf of both HR and the business to drive effective people performance as something of a life calling. If this is ingrained into our very being then very little will serve to change this constant posture in us.

Therefore, if this is our vocation, changing jobs or being promoted beyond the role will make us no less an HR business partner. We will still continue to think and act like people-expert HR business partners.

Proactively deciding to move beyond our vocation could be a challenging one. It may even cause us to question whether this was in fact our vocation after all. Nevertheless, many of us will attempt to take on this vocational challenge and grapple with this concept of promotion beyond our vocation.

Personally, I have had, and will in future have, many different job titles but I am, and always will be, an HR business partner at heart.

Particularly problematic promotions

When considering the trajectory of a successful HR business partner, maybe it is a very natural and redeemable thought that the most senior HR generalist is the type of person we would want to lead the entire HR function. If this person has proven to be competent in business partnering and, perhaps, they have mastered all the principles in this book and much more, then surely they would be a natural and compelling candidate for leading the entire HR function. This route of promotion is well trodden, and I think well recognized within our profession.

Personally, I am biased, but I would see the promotion of a person like this as a loss to the HR business partnering function, not a gain to the HR function or organization. I know that is a sweeping statement and to some may sound a little contrived or self-serving (especially having just warned about HR infighting in Chapter 16!). However, my focus in this book is firmly on the discipline of HR business partnering. In matters of HR business partnering I will confess to taking a purist approach and I am prepared to be called closed-minded if it is ultimately in the pursuit of the enlargement of the auspices of the HR business partner. Also, let me say for the final time, please remember that I am prone to exaggerate for effect if I think it will help bring us closer to a truth.

Primarily though, by making this point, I want to relieve successful individuals from the feeling that we must be promoted further to progress.

Having been promoted to the role of HR business partner, further promotion will be right for some, but I have come to discover that, for most, promotion is not necessarily the cure for that itch. Specifically, what seems to be a natural promotion to lead the HR function, the roles of head of HR or HR director, can be particularly problematic.

Whether we think it of our own accord, or we are told it erroneously, a role that is accountable for leading the entire breadth of HR professionals employed, and HR services offered by an organization, is a very different ball game from the, at times, individualistic role we have come to master. It is a bigger leap than it may appear. The size and scale of the organization will usually have a direct impact on the magnitude of the leap. Nevertheless, there is a significant gap between where we are and leading the entire HR function. Even at a much-reduced scale, the focus and requirements of the lead HR role within an organization are wholly different to a senior and strategic HR business partner role. We should not blindly assume that a step down in size and scale, or perhaps a change of sector, will make the role of leading the HR function easier or the transition more straight forward. Leading the HR function is a very different proposition to a career of blissful HR business partnering.

Obviously, I am not saying it is impossible, and in some cases right, for a someone to make this transition to leading the entire HR function, I am just trying to *relieve* most of us from believing this is our necessary future calling in life. I want to relieve us of this because I have definitely experienced a pre-programmed thinking that our next natural progression is to lead the HR function. Maybe this has something to do with usually being ranked amongst the most senior members of the function, or already holding director-level relationships across the organization. These factors will certainly ease the transition to a more senior role but do not compel us to have to take this step.

Perhaps it is the kudos associated with the title, the position, of 'head of' or 'director of' the profession, something that speaks to the pride in all of us. This pride could cause us to fail to accurately assess what we really want, and instead cause us to pursue something even though it may cause us pain and anxiety. What most of us are so desperately seeking in these moments is progression and not promotion. If the allure of the title is irresistible the fear of losing it once attained is even greater. An error of judgement in accepting a promotion is made worse by the fact that once we have a hold of something, we tend not to want to let it go, or be seen to lose it. We most definitely do not want to be seen to be stepping back down to a perceived 'lower' role in either organizational or CV terms. Making the wrong decision may cause some pain, but in this case undoing it will require real courage and a good deal more pain.

Whatever is causing this trend, my aim here is to release us to think not so much about promotion but instead more holistically about progression and a type of sustainable longevity. Our careers are likely to be long, which should cause us to give more attention to decisions that present us with a sustainable path. Longevity in the profession is a difficult trait to actively cultivate but choosing sustainable routes will enable us to avoid becoming discouraged, stuck or regretful over time. I believe the key to this is to understand what we *really* want. To do so requires us to consider progression not promotion, and not just what the current circumstances or cultural norms may seek to set and impose upon us.

Know what you want

We seldom truly know the answer to this question of what we want, especially if asked directly. Too often our corporate environments only breed robotic thinkers who just want what the last person had, almost as if a perceived rite of passage will somehow be fulfilling. Brilliant people with huge potential can easily be reduced to only desiring their line manager's role. This is another strange phenomenon of human behaviour: how can something that was right for one person be right for all the people always? Not enough serious thought has been done in this area of understanding what we each really want. If we can identify what we *really* want, we will at least have some realistic chance of achieving it and experiencing the gratifying peace that comes when we love what we do.

A lack of serious consideration in this area will lead to flawed decision making. This deficiency will cause us to become susceptible to suggestion, thereby risking an undesired association with the common magpie – chasing after anything shiny that appears on the horizon. Many of us will discover that our first task in deciphering what we really want is to resist this tendency to chase anything shiny that is dangled in front of us.

To limit oneself to only thinking about the next job title, as opposed to the type of work one really wants to do, is misguided and short-sighted.

Knowing what we really want is deeply personal. It is likely to be influenced by our own life and career experiences and current environmental factors, which will be unique to each of us. Expert career coaching aside, it is for these reasons I believe we should resist the suggestions of others when understanding what *we* really want and need.

To stand still is to go backwards

I wish here that I had the experience to provide a neat formula for discerning what progression looks like for each of us, such that we avoid making these mistakes of promotion. Understanding what each of us needs to progress and sustain our success and happiness is a difficult task. It is a difficult task to determine for ourselves, let alone for me to attempt to determine it for you.

It is a sad fact that there comes a point where people fail in truly understanding what they want and instead turn to counting down the years, or counting up the pension pot, as a route to secure current motivation based on future, and not present, happiness. This practice is a kind of potential-limiting trade off, which personally I have never been prepared to accept.

All I can say is that the search for our own progression may not be a linear one, you might have to first see something, or try something, to know if you are going to find happiness in doing it. I have encountered many people who claim to have 'fallen into HR', and seem perfectly happy about it. By the same token I think it is ok to 'fall' in and out of opportunities that may provide true progression.

The best advice I can give is to be continually committed to trying different things and taking on new challenges. When we stop trying new things and being challenged by our day-to-day, we will find that our own personal and professional development will stagnate. There is no faster route to misery and staleness than standing still. Standing still whilst the rest of the world is moving forwards will mean that we are effectively going backwards. There is really no such thing as standing still. There is only forward or back.

Taking these small everyday risks to try different roles across the HR profession, and more widely across the spectrum of disciplines within an organization, will enable you to learn what progression really looks like for you. Never settle for the status quo for too long, it will be the slow death of your motivation. A career can span 40-plus years, which seems like a long time, but it is too short to spend *any* time bored, unhappy or unfulfilled in what you do. We must all take progression seriously.

In pursuit of progression I have tried many things, I have had some success and some failure, plenty of false starts, sideways steps and more than one backward step. It has been anything but a straight-line of promotion.

Many people have supported me on this journey, many made valid suggestions, provided information, coaching, advice, challenge, opportunity, as well as contacts for me to network with. But ultimately, through all of this, no one could make the decision for me about what it was that *I* wanted to do – about what would make me happy and provide me with progression. That privilege lies solely in the eye of the beholder. This question will be of utmost importance to our future success. We must know what we want; our continued progression relies on it.

Never give up

Wherever you find yourself on the journey of HR business partnering, and wherever you place on this spectrum between progression and promotion, always remember one thing: this working life is a tough one – it will beat us up, throw us out and put us down – but it can never stop us achieving our own self-defined progression.

You will be sure to encounter moments where people tell you it is all over, or you may yourself conclude that everything you built has all come tumbling down, but I did not write this whole book to end it by endorsing the mediocrity of our failed ambition. It is only over when you say it is. People can block your promotion, but they cannot stop your self-appointed path of progression.

Understanding what you want and seeking after that will lead you places you could never imagine or wish for. It will be a kind of peace and calm that is seldom uncovered in the workplace. Being comfortable letting others climb the greasy pole, whilst you seek out the latest twist and turn of your own single-track road, contains the kind of fulfilment that money cannot buy.

Your path is individual to you, you are unique in your thoughts, preferences, motivations and desires. You will mark out your own path through a progression that leads to your personal peace and happiness. There is no reason for you to follow the crowd and seek out what others claimed to find fulfilling or necessary.

Over time I have learnt to resist the system, to refrain from playing the games set out for us. I hope in this book I have given you the tools to be successful, discover your vocation and, ultimately, to forge your own path.

Finally, I say all of this because I have the best job in HR, and I want you to have it too.

Summary

In summary, it is possible that some of us might suffer from the effects of having ambitious but ultimately limited aspirations. We see ahead to the future but perhaps not far enough or not quite the whole picture. So, once we have achieved our aim of becoming an HR business partner and mastering the role, we are unsure as to what our next career step should be. We will have to consider whether it is enough *just* to be a great HR business partner. Therefore, I want to relieve successful individuals of the feeling that we must be promoted further to progress. There can be an allure that comes with promotion – a more senior role, position and job title – but these things alone won't be sufficient to guarantee our progression or secure our workplace happiness. Promotion may of course be right for some, but it should not necessarily be our default setting. To successfully navigate this challenge, we must truly know what we really want. We have to resist the temptation to simply desire the role of our line manager as our next career progression step. A lack of serious consideration in this area will lead to flawed decision making. Knowing what we really want is deeply personal and is likely to be influenced by our own life and career experiences. The search for our own progression may not be a linear one, it may involve trying and failing many times over before we discover the kind of progression that brings us purpose and happiness. The key is to ensure that we are not standing still in our pursuit for progression. Never settle for the status quo for too long. Never give up.

Epilogue

Don't stay too long

If you must play, decide on three things at the start: the rules of the game, the stakes and the quitting time.

CHINESE PROVERB

I have quit three jobs and been fired from most of the rest. Getting fired, despite sometimes coming as a surprise and leaving you scrambling to recover, is often a godsend: Someone else makes the decision for you, and it's impossible to sit in the wrong job for the rest of your life. Most people aren't lucky enough to get fired and die a slow spiritual death over 30–40 years of tolerating the mediocre.

TIMOTHY FERRISS (2007)

The six-year rule

Susie had been working in HR for nearly four years. It was her first proper job. She was excited to take on her very first HR role and make the transition from full-time education into the big wide world of work. She had originally joined the HR team as an administrator, the most junior role within the function, working closely with the recruitment team. She had quickly progressed from there through various temporary roles within the HR team before successfully landing a junior advisor role within the HR business partnering team. With four years of institutional knowledge under her belt she was beginning to grow in confidence in her role.

Despite her ever-growing experience Susie was still young, in her very early twenties and had precious little workplace knowledge to draw on aside from the experience of Saturday jobs when she was at college. She was youngest person on her team, and felt the weight of being the least experienced. Susie was bright and a quick learner, but her youth brought with it a precociousness that at times got her into awkward spots with more mature and professional colleagues. Inevitably, her decision-making skills were also still somewhat under-developed, and she needed coaching from her colleagues to reach the right decision. Despite this, she had a huge amount of potential that was evident to others and she was keen to learn and progress her HR career.

Each working day presented a steep learning curve and many everyday occurrences, and of course people, made a great impression upon Susie. Not least of these people was her HR director at the time, the only HR director she had ever known, a gentle and wise man named Peter.

Peter, over the preceding four-year period, had always proved to be thoughtful, wise and patient with all kinds of people, especially with one precocious teenage upstart. Susie suspected that these were the essential features that make up a well-liked and respected HR director. Peter had grown up within the organization and had spent the preceding 37 years employed there. He had achieved incredible progression over that time, going from the young trainee to eventually leading the entire HR function. Quite literally man and boy. This caught Susie's attention because Peter had joined the organization at the same age she did, albeit 30-something years earlier. In her youth and general workplace naivety she could not begin to comprehend what she thought about this, whether it was good, bad or indifferent. She couldn't imagine Peter much younger than he was now, and so it seemed as though he must have occupied the position of HR director for the entire 37 years!

However, his story gave her something to aspire to. The idea that he started out in HR at the same age she did, also in the most junior of roles, to then go on to be the HR director was an inspiring story that gave hope for her future career aspirations. This fact, coupled with Peter's generosity with his time, had helped Susie and Peter form a strong connection and working relationship.

For Susie, as a young person joining the organization with no experience in a corporate workplace or office environment, it proved to be a fascinating place to work. The thing Susie found to be most remarkable was, back then, the working environment was almost entirely governed by personalities.

In terms of how decisions were made there was little notion of organizational design as a discipline, and the concepts informing decision-making did not appear to be applied within the organization at that time. Instead, Susie slowly discovered that everything was run on soft power. If she wanted to get something done, she had to figure out who the one person was who could unlock it for her. It was highly dysfunctional, but somehow simultaneously effective once she knew her way around the people and their quirky personas. Susie had a natural and genuine interest in people, and this, coupled with the enthusiasm of youth, was like a kind of volatile science experiment involving real-world examples and real people!

The organization was made up of around 5000 people, and as the HR director, Peter presided over them all and the vagaries of their personality-led approach to the world of work. Set against the myriad of weird and wonderful personalities, Peter proved to be something of a calming influence, a kind of true north in a sea of unpredictability. He was often the most senior person in the room, and always the humblest. He was held in high regard by all who knew him and worked with him.

One day, without warning and entirely out of the blue, after 37 long years of loyal service, Peter announced his sudden retirement. He was only around 56 years old at the time.

As a very young and inexperienced person, this announcement had a big impact on Susie. Not least because she just did not see it coming. It was a complete shock to her, a total surprise. But, as Susie learned, apparently *no one* had seen this one coming. This was not in the plan and had come to pass several years before anyone was expecting it to.

Peter was responsible for leading a large part-decentralized HR function of around 80 people, so his sudden resignation and retirement directly and indirectly affected a lot of people and had wide-ranging consequences. The shock waves across the organization were palpable, and naturally the scramble had begun to consider who would replace him in this high-powered and important role.

Bereft of answers and desperate to know more, one evening Susie intentionally hung back until most everyone had left the building, but typically Peter was still in his corner office with the light on, the winter darkness drawing in.

Susie slunk into his office for what she thought was a very natural and subtle 'have you got a minute?' chat. With the benefit of immediate hindsight, she realized that at such an early stage in her career, and in her obvious naivety, she would have lacked the necessary tact to pull this subtlety off without her true motive going undetected by Peter's sageness. He nodded, sanguine in the knowledge of what was coming next. Susie sat down in his office and asked him something along the lines of the inevitable 'so how come you're leaving?'.

Ever generous with his time, Peter paused and looked carefully at Susie to check she was really listening. He then began by explaining how he and his mother had recently attended the funeral of a distant family member. Susie, in her impatience was immediately perplexed by this story, and quickly began to think, 'Why are you telling me this?'. However, all would become clear. Peter explained that at this family funeral, his mother and he had been remembering the other male members of his family who were no longer living. In considering these lost loved ones, they came to the revelation that *none* of the male members of Peter's family had lived beyond the age of approximately 62. Peter, at 56, was preciously close to this apparently deadly age.

Peter explained that realizing this fact was enough for him to decide to completely give up work and retire with immediate effect.

For Susie, understanding his reasoning was enlightening and it was surprising to hear him talk so candidly about such morbid events. However, the conversation continued, and it was what Peter said next that forever changed Susie's approach to her HR career and outlook on her future progression. Peter's next words were to stay with her in a very simple but deeply profound way. As ever, thinking not only of himself, Peter saw an opportunity to impart some wisdom – reflecting on his full 37 years of service, he said to Susie:

Whatever you do, never stay anywhere for more than six years, everything will just repeat itself in six-year cycles. After six years or so, new people come along with new ideas which you come to realize are actually just the old ideas that you've seen before but repackaged to look new.

This was a particularly stark statement for someone who, contrary to the advice given, had remained in-situ for a total of 37 years. A period of no less than six of these six-year cycles that he was warning against.

Coming from someone Susie trusted deeply, and given she was only three or four years into the first organization of her long HR career, this was advice she took to heart and heeded.

Quitting time

Whether we agree or not, the story of Susie and Peter provides many lessons for all of us. Firstly, from Susie's perspective, it reminds us of the importance of giving careful consideration to who we listen to and take advice from throughout our careers. Secondly, from Peter's perspective, it is a timely reminder that our words can have a great effect on people, and as such we should be deliberate and careful before we speak.

One of the beauties of what we do in HR is that we can pick it up and take it anywhere. Any organization employing even a modest number of people is very likely to have a dedicated HR function. Industry knowledge can be important and relevant in moving between organizations, but herein lies the unassailable truth about HR – people are the same wherever we work.

Organizations always speak of having unique challenges but, in reality, there are very few truly unique situations that the HR profession has not seen or experienced somewhere before. For accountants, numbers add up the same wherever they choose to work; the same principle rings true for HR and people.

This creates many fantastic opportunities out there for a competent HR professional. If we were to use Peter's words to guide our own approach to 'quitting time' we will discover many new and exciting opportunities available to us throughout our careers.

Of course, Peter's words cannot be applied as an arbitrary rule and no resignations have ever been tendered because an artificial time limit has been reached. Moreover, those words were spoken in a different time and were referring to an even earlier time in the late 20th century. So, we must add a pinch of modern thought to this historically sage offering. Even so, I would still advocate the spirit of this six-year rule when we are considering our options for progression.

As you have hopefully figured out by now, I care about people. I hope that I do have a genuine interest in people in line with what I have described throughout these pages. It is for these reasons that I hate to see 'stuck' people who have long since overstayed this six-year rule (keep in mind that not everyone who has stayed longer than six years is stuck!). Over the course of our careers we are likely to encounter many people who have simply stayed too long at one organization and become 'stuck' in this way. Their stories will be similar – there was a point where longevity brought them success, but overstaying has meant that sustained success has passed them by. Instead, in these latter years they find they are accompanied by weariness, occasionally bitterness and a definite sense of going into battle each day. These are often the people who were not 'lucky enough to get fired'.

Whilst it is not an exact science, I do believe that the consideration of tenure in roles and stays at organizations in *maximum* six-year blocks will help to keep the mind fresh and the heart free. Many people will find an optimum length of stay to be far shorter, and others perhaps somewhat longer. Personally, I would say that there is little worse than overstaying your welcome and then discovering that you are entirely stuck somewhere you should have left behind long ago.

The stories we tell

Peter's HR career may have concluded many years ago, but much like the example of the legacy left by Jimmy V at the beginning of this book, it is his words that continue to live on and stand the test of time to the benefit of those willing to listen.

Between us all we will have thousands of different experiences and millions of different stories to tell. Each of these individual stories will have the power to change the lives of specific people at key moments in their careers. I've used my own story to build something in this book that I hope can help as many people as possible in ways unique to their needs. In reading my story I hope it helps you begin to appreciate the power you have in your own hands. I hope it inspires you to start to tell your story too; it could change someone's life.

My only hope is that my words and actions could one day have a lasting and positive effect on someone else's life. After all, isn't that what human resources is all about?

Reference

Ferriss, T (2007) *The 4-Hour Work Week: Escape the 9–5, live anywhere and join the new rich*, Crown Publishers, New York

ACKNOWLEDGEMENTS

Writing a book like this at a natural inflection point in my own career has caused me to consider who I really ought to thank, and most importantly, what it was that those people gave me or taught me.

There have been many people who have been part of my HR journey who I have enjoyed working with and who have made my working life a little brighter and a little more fun. I am grateful for all of you. I hope here to acknowledge those who made it possible for me to be able to write this book.

Starting at the beginning, I have to thank my parents, Paula Morrison and Michael Templeman, for supporting my decision to drop-out of college after only a few weeks to try to 'get a job in HR'. Things worked out well in the end!

I owe a debt of thanks to Pat Penniston and Angela Claridge for taking a chance on me as a 16-year-old and giving me the first opportunity, which ultimately became the foundation of my whole career.

To the original employee relations dream team, Hilary Beaumont, Sean McCarthy, Claire Richardson and Louise Manley, you all taught me so much about HR, people and the world of work. I will be forever grateful for your endless patience and your willingness to teach and correct me at every turn. Sometimes I think that everything I know was learnt from you. I am also eternally grateful for Alan Buttery's leadership, which had a profound effect on me in my formative years.

I need to thank Michael Carling for believing in me and giving me an opportunity at just the right moment.

I'm grateful to my friend David Robinson for showing me that it was possible to write a professional book about what you do.

Sarah Stacey gave me the job I had spent my whole career working towards (my first bona fide HR business partner role) and backed me to deliver in challenging times.

Mike Culver and Pete Bull both brought sense to madness, placed their trust in me and were bold enough to give me significant opportunities which became career highlights.

Rich Morris taught me everything I know about programme management and was gracious enough to continue helping me long after.

Julie Foy picked me up when I was down and looked past my own diva behaviour to help to resurrect my HR career when I was unsure of the next steps. Her leadership is a great example to me and many others.

Similarly, Grace Christie took the time to dust me off and support me to find those crucial next steps at a key moment in my personal work life journey.

The intentional, timely and precise praise of Tim Johnson always let me know that my natural abilities were recognized and valued.

A special thanks must go to Andrea Dhillon and Ruth Johnson who both helped me to hone the early parts of this book and without whom there may not have been a book at all. This book is for both of you and I hope it helps you to get where you're going.

I am grateful to those who took the time to read chapters of the book during its creation. Claire Wildman, James Eales, Helen Lutton, Joel Soares, Shehani Goonesekera, Dan Prideaux and Amelia Vinnell, your feedback and encouragement helped to transform words on a page into living breathing ideas.

I am particularly indebted to Josh Walton who read an entire draft and diligently noted for me his feedback on each section and the book as a whole.

I want to thank everyone at Kogan Page who has made this book a reality. Especially my commissioning editor Lucy Carter, who had the vision for this book way before I did and championed it from day one. Also, to my development editor Anne-Marie Heeney for reading every word and graciously entertaining my queries about the inclusion of rap music lyrics as epigraphs.

Also, I could not have completed this process without friends like Isaac Borquaye who have gone ahead of me and blazed the trail.

Across the length of a career there are some people who give you opportunity, others who teach you, and then there are those who get you through it all and without whom you just couldn't have done it. Natalie Horsfield, Kate Snell, Laura Klose, Lisa Archer, Graham Hopper, Antoinette Aylett, Elaine Chapman, Lindsay Mosuro, Sara Mirza, Helen Lutton, Russell Veale, Helen Zambuni, you were and are those people for me!

Finally, I want to thank my wife Chloe who is TBE, my PIC and fellow dreamer, without whom this book could not have been conceived.

INDEX

Printed in the USA
CPSIA information can be obtained
at www.ICGtesting.com
CBHW070826180224
4401CB00075B/1274